A LONG WAY FROM HOME

A LONG WAY FROM HOME

A Sociological Exploration of Contemporary Idolatry

J. A. WALTER

Exeter
The Paternoster Press

AUSTRALIA:
Emu Book Agencies Pty., Ltd.,
63, Berry St., Granville, 2142, N.S.W.

SOUTH AFRICA:
Oxford University Press,
P.O. Box 1141, Cape Town

British Library Cataloguing in Publication Data

Walter, J A
A long way from home
1. Sociology, Christian 2. Civilization, Occidental
I. Title
261 BT738

ISBN 0–85364–259–1
ISBN 0–85364–260–5 Pbk

Typeset by Input Typesetting Ltd
and Printed in Great Britain for The Paternoster Press,
Paternoster House, 3 Mount Radford Crescent, Exeter, Devon
by Redwood Burn Ltd, Trowbridge & Esher

Contents

Preface

The reader should be forewarned that this book draws on two traditions which are not normally found explicitly within the covers of one book – the Judaic-Christian and sociological traditions. This may mean that readers number both sociologists and Christians; I crave indulgence from sociologist readers for some rather parochial theological and churchly asides, and from Christian readers for a few academic sociological asides. Hopefully though, the sociology and the theology are complementary and essential aspects of the same argument.

In attempting to bring together sociology and theology I have been much encouraged by the writings of Jacques Ellul and Peter Berger. Rather than acknowledge on every other page their influence, it is better to state my indebtedness right at the beginning. Some of their works are cited in the section on 'further reading' at the end of the book.

I am also indebted to Peter Cousins, Peter McCaffery, Keith White and Os Guinness for helpfully commenting on a draft manuscript. A big thank-you also to several members of the Ilkley Study Group for their support and stimulation over the past seven years; in particular, Howard Davis, Rob Furbey, David Lyon and Godfrey Williams may recognise some of their ideas (doubtless mutilated) reappearing within these covers. Responsibility for the final product is, of course, mine.

Some of the thinking behind the book was forged in (sometimes vehement) discussions with my father, who I hope does not see them as entirely fruitless; also in discussion with Kingston Kajese, whose willingness to listen and criticise has been a constant support.

Despite critical comments in ch. 2, I should add that I am indebted also to the British social security system for keeping body and mind together while the book was being written.

1
A Secular Society?

Sociologists, theologians and more ordinary mortals rarely have much time for each other; on those rare occasions when they do, they are unlikely to understand, let alone agree with, one another. But there is one thing on which there seems near unanimous agreement: that ours is a secular age. The sociologist includes 'secularisation' in the battery of theories by which he or she claims to clarify (others would say mystify) what is going on in modern society; theologians proclaim God to be dead and Man to have come of age in a world which is now thoroughly demythologised; and the man in the street backs all this up by claiming to have little interest in religion. Humanists are overjoyed at this spectacle of secularisation, while the majority of Christians (those, that is, who do not read the trendy theologians) bemoan it. But they all agree that secularisation has occurred, or is occurring.

True, some sociologists spend much time and energy discussing the nature of secularisation. They wrangle over how to define it[1], they speculate on its meaning and causes[2], and they spend their research grants attempting to measure how far secularisation has proceeded and whether or not the latest esoteric cults constitute a hiccup in this inexorable process[3]. But very few sociologists doubt that the very notion of secularisation makes sense in itself[4], nor do they doubt that it makes sense of what is happening to contemporary religion and society. In this respect, sociologists are loyal followers of one of their nineteenth century founding fathers, Auguste Comte, who thought that civilisation was evolving inevitably along a road from primitive religion to a 'positive' era of scientific humanism in which religion and metaphysics are banished to the land of myth and fantasy where they belong.

It is this almost universally accepted notion that society is becoming progressively less religious that this book is dedicated to challenging.

This is not to deny that there have been important historical changes in religion and belief. Certainly the institutional church is not the proud flagship of the cultural fleet that once she was. Ever since the middle ages, there have been increasingly successful attacks on Christendom – on the subjection of the whole of society to the church and its beliefs. With the Reformation, the Enlightenment, the emergence of science and the modern nation-state, more and more areas of life have been wrested away from the church, leaving it with control and authority over an ever decreasing area so that now the church has authority only over the private domain of personal morality[5]. This is a process as Bryan Wilson puts it, 'whereby religious thinking, practice and institutions lose their social significance'[6]: the church is now of *personal significance only*, and to a minority at that.

Certainly, too, belief in the supernatural is on the wane[7]. People are more and more concerned with life in this world rather than in the hereafter, and society is not pervaded with spirits and demons, witches and hobgoblins as in medieval Europe or in traditional tribal societies today. If the supernatural does exist, it exists 'out there' and there is a big gulf between it and the here and now.

But can we be said to live in a secular society if, even with the decline of the institutional church and of belief in the supernatural, there is evidence that *the sacred* still occupies a central place in society? The sacred has been an essential ingredient of all religions, and indeed of all known societies, up to the present time. In the Greek and Christian influenced history of western Europe and America[8], the sacred has been composed of two elements.

Firstly, the sacred is or represents an object of worship, of ultimate worth, to which people are committed and which forms their ultimate concern[9]. Of course, in all religions the sacred is far from being in the forefront of everyone's mind during every waking moment, but so long as it continues to form the context within which life is oriented then it is still sacred[10].

Secondly, the sacred is a source of absolute meaning that provides believers with a validated place in the scheme of things. It provides an ordered world in which people belong[11]; it relates them to the rest of the universe and to the non-human world; and it injects meaning into life which enables them to make sense of and endure suffering, death and undeserved evil[12]. In a religious world, life is not meaningless; it is rich with meaning, replete with symbols and myths of good and evil.

In addition to providing an object of worship and a home in the universe, the sacred integrates life for both individual and society. The ultimate commitment and the pervasiveness of meaning serve to hold together the different arenas of life; indeed the sacred is the very cement of society[13].

Society can be said to have ceased to be religious only if there is no longer any evidence of the sacred. So the question is, are there present in modern society things for which people live, to which they are ultimately committed, which provide life with meaning, and which integrate the variety of human experience?

The answer is manifestly, 'Yes'. Take the family. It is an ultimate concern for which people drop, and are expected to drop, other commitments when they get married and again when they have children. It provides life with meaning in that husbands not only put up with alienating and dehumanising jobs for the sake of their families, but even imbue such jobs with meaning and worth; similarly wives put up with the drudgeries of the kitchen for the sake of the family, and even find these drudgeries meaningful. The family also focuses the different concerns of its individual members: the tedium of work, struggling with the income tax form, joining a local environmental group, or getting the baby baptised all make sense when done for the sake of the family and the future of the children. The family is also one of the very few things to which people are so dedicated that they are prepared to suffer and die; for the sake of their children men can fairly easily be persuaded into fighting wars and many women to endure insufferable conditions; thus certain forms of suffering and death are legitimised by the family. Thus it exhibits all the characteristics of the sacred.

But there are certain kinds of death with which the family cannot cope. When a loved one, especially a child, dies, the bereaved often feel there is nothing left to live for and that life has become meaningless. The routines of everyday living may continue, but mechanically and without commitment because nothing seems to hang together any more. When people lose their family or important members of it, they react as though the focus of their life and their ultimate concern has been taken from them. The same experience of emptiness may occur even if a child has not died but has simply grown up and left home; the centre, the sacred, of the mother's life has vanished and she feels empty.

The family is sacred not only for private individuals but also for public spokesmen. In the year of writing (1978), both the British Prime Minister and the Leader of the Opposition described the family as 'sacred' and advocated measures to uphold it. Its centrality is also embedded in social institutions: the law, the tax and social security systems, building society and life insurance policies, advertising and television programming can only operate by recognising the centrality of the family in modern society.

So today's family is sacred. (Lest it be objected that the family has always been central to society, it is worth reading a little about its history in Europe[14] or a little anthropology, and it will become apparent that the idea of the family has not always been so important.) A little further investigation would show that it is not just the family that displays the characteristics of the sacred. Work, individuality, science, politics and the idea of progress are all sacreds that provide meaning and demand commitment from both society and individual. The loss or undermining of any of these is a catastrophe that is comparable only to loss of religious faith: widespread disillusion and a sense of dislocation accompany unemployment, the erosion of a person's individuality, or the undermining of the myth that Science and Politics can deliver the goods of eternal Progress, (as with the nuclear threat in the '50s, the Vietnam War in the '60s and Watergate in the '70s).

A major aim of this book is to provide evidence that the sacred remains an essential (but undesirable) part of modern society. Certain definable sacreds still enable people to make sense of and endure their otherwise somewhat miserable lot on this earth. Such an analysis of the sacred owes much to Karl Marx who understood this when he described religion as 'the opium of the people'; the sacred provides (illegitimate) answers to the pain of human existence and blinds human beings to the need for radical change. The analysis differs from Marx, though, in the radical change envisaged.

This book also owes much to another great social theorist, Emile Durkheim, who understood the inextricable relationship between the sacred and society itself. Durkheim claimed that religion could only be understood as a social phenomenon, and he strongly hinted that the reverse is also true, that society can only be fully understood as a religious phenomenon[15]. An implication of this (which the agnostic Durkheim would not consider) is that in order to understand society we need a theology as well as a sociology. In its early days in the nineteenth century, sociology rightly freed itself from the religious worldview of a church that proved itself incapable of comprehending the world-shattering events of the industrial, political and intellectual revolutions of that century. Sociology's mistake, though, was to suppose that it could dispense with all kinds of religious understanding and still produce a total picture of society. An aim of this book, then, is to insert sociology within a broader Christian framework, although this framework will remain largely implicit until the last chapter. One idea that will be referred to throughout, however, has explicit Judaic-Christian connotations, and to this idea of 'idolatry' we will now briefly turn.

Aspects of the Sacred

Since the sacred is the central idea in this book, let us explore its characteristics further, under the four headings of *idolatry*, *homelessness*, *nature* and *mortality*.

Idolatry

The granting of ultimate worth to the sacred and making it an ultimate concern will frequently be termed 'idolatry' in this book. The word 'idol' means 'an object of love, admiration, or honour in an extreme degree' (*Chambers Twentieth Century Dictionary*), but it also implies a *false* object, not worthy of such admiration. The introduction of this highly evaluative term into the discussion is valid both within the Judaic-Christian framework in which only God himself is worthy of worship and anything else commanding ultimate commitment is a false god or idol; and within the humanist framework in which all meaning is humanly created and to set human constructions up as absolute and external to man (and hence alien to him) is to commit the cardinal sin of alienation. Marx's idea of the sacred as alienation, as a projection into the void of man's own activities and concerns, has strong links with the condemnation of idolatry by the Old Testament prophets[16].

Although idols are worshipped personally by individuals, as in Ancient Israel, they are also a thoroughly *sociological* phenomenon. Individuals do not simply pluck out of thin air the particular idols that they wish to worship; they are members of a society which has set up public shrines and altars at which people are either invited or cajoled into worshipping. The individual today may conceivably worship any god he wishes, but he or she lives in a society in which public shrines are set up to some gods and not to others, and it takes a brave or original person to absent himself from these and set up his own. People select their idols from the limited range on offer in the supermarket of society.

This book is not primarily about idolatry as practised by individuals; some individuals are mad about golf, others about stamp collecting, and still others about Humphrey Bogart films, but these are rarely idols in the sense that they integrate the whole of the person's life and they are certainly not societal idols for there are no pressures on people generally to worship at these shrines. These are merely personal fads. The sacred, by contrast, involves the elevation of a particular social institution or idea to such a level within a culture that it forms a major and indispensable part of people's identity. Patriotism in the Third Reich illustrates this. Patriotism can be a good thing, but when it is made the highest value to which all other values are subordinated, then it becomes sacred. Here we are not talking about the over-patriotic crank in an otherwise more balanced society, but about the kind of patriotism that existed in Nazi Germany where patriotism was primarily a societal and only secondarily an individually held value. It was the Nazi *culture* that made patriotism sacred; it was the culture that provided the altars at which individuals subsequently bowed.

It is perhaps easy to identify the sacred in another country and time, but more difficult to identify it in our own society today because we ourselves invoke the sacred and believe our own gods to be not idols but true, honourable and real. It is easy enough to identify someone else's odd fads; much more difficult to discern the spirits which pervade the very cultural air we breathe.

This game of idol-spotting has to be done with care. Although anything *can* become sacred, it is not every idea and institution that actually *is* sacred. What distinguishes one society from another is *which* shrines are set up, although there is a tendency for all modern industrial societies to elevate the same ones. Every society is idolatrous in that it raises some ideas and institutions to the level of a religious absolute, but which particular altars are set up can vary widely. Although a society believes its shrines to be sacred and its altars to be absolute, they have in fact been chosen in the highly relative circumstances of culture and history. Thus Mao's China, urgently needing to feed its people and form a base for economic development, chose to sacralise (among other things) work. Many western nations did much the same in the early stages of their industrialisation.

Also, different sections of society may worship at different altars. Certain sacreds may be held in common, but within this community wide differences can co-exist. The values of one social class, ethnic group, or subculture may directly conflict with those of other groups, even though the dominant group may do its best to impose a cultural sameness throughout society, either consciously through propaganda or unconsciously through de facto control of the mass media, education, advertising, politics and other opinion-forming institutions[17].

An idol is not in itself bad for, since anything can be idolised, this would make the whole material and social world utterly bad and irredeemable, which is certainly not the Judaic-Christian position implicit in this book (although gnostic heresies have from time to time tended to this position). Rather, an idol is something which is good in itself but which becomes evil and alienating when set up as the highest good and as a religious absolute. Thus, both democracy and socialism are often believed in as absolutes rather than as fallible yet more or less useful humanly-devised political arrangements. Similarly, the modern form of family life is believed to be sacred rather than simply a particular historical development; rather than being simply part of the good life, modern romantic and parental love claim to *be* the good life.

Each of the other three characteristics of the sacred are attempts to solve fundamental problems which seem inevitably to accompany the human condition. These problems are far from finally solved, and as a result the present century sees new sacreds being set up to cope with these typically human problems:–

Homelessness

Traditionally, the sacred insists on a place for the individual within the community, and for the community within the universe. It affords a framework of meaning which provides a shelter from the possibility of life falling apart and disintegrating into a nightmare. Because of the threat of meaninglessness, man is forced to relate himself to some entity which in its absoluteness is capable of overcoming meaninglessness[18]. The sacred takes the fragility of human existence and gives it solidity; it takes the frailty of reality and makes it massive. In Peter Berger's term, it provides a 'sacred canopy'[19].

The canopy provided by the sacreds of traditional society was so secure that the frailty underlying reality rarely surfaced. But the old canopy is now in tatters. The decline of Christendom, of the institutional church and its stable view of the world, has left modern man peculiarly homeless. In Christendom, people were able to place themselves in relation to the Christian God who was conceived (among other things) as the Creator of the universe; people thus had a place in the cosmic order of things and were at home in the universe. When God 'died', with the end of societal validation of his existence, Man became as it were a wanderer on the face of the earth, alone in the universe. With no external deity and no revelation to provide values, norms and guidelines for life, mankind had to start from scratch and build its own home. The philosophers of the eighteenth century Enlightenment realised this when they argued that society has to draw up its own *contrat social* by which it can determine how it should order itself and how its members should live. But the result of their efforts at desacralising the cosmos was the elevation of new sacreds: the individual, the nation-state, politics, and science.

It is not just religious change that has made modern man homeless. More important perhaps are the social changes of the last four centuries: The ending of feudal society and its replacement with various kinds of capitalism and socialism; the trickle and then the flood of people migrating from traditional rural life to the cosmopolitan, free and anonymous city; the replacement of subsistence farming and small family workshops by large scale industry – all these have transformed what was once the human home into something that was, to the first migrants, altogether unrecognisable.

These social changes were sometimes intricately linked with religious change. In the transition from the medieval to the modern world, the social changes created a climate in which new religious ideas developed. At the same time, these new ideas actually accelerated social change: the Reformation and Puritanism in particular seem to have been influential in promoting business enterprise and science[20].

The most dramatic resurgences of the sacred are to be found where this homelessness is most acute today. In South Africa, for example, black migrants to the towns, culturally homeless and separated from their families and roots in the homelands, form a ready clientèle for new fundamentalist sects which offer a new home in heaven. Or to take a very different example, it was in the economically chaotic Germany of the 1920s where the middle class in particular felt its security slipping away that the typically modern sacred of nationalism took its most virulent form; and it is in the culturally disrupted countries of the Third World that today nationalism has its greatest appeal.

This problem of homelessness has been the theme of much twentieth century thought. Existentialism has stressed the need for the individual to create his own meaning out of the absurdity and meaninglessness of existence. Sociologists have pointed out that the most effective solutions to homelessness are those that are backed up by social institutions and are communally accepted; the individual choosing his own meaning has a tough time unless his choice is confirmed by society. If the reality constructed by the individual does not mesh with social reality, for example if he believes himself to be Napoleon Bonaparte whereas society believes him to be Joe Bloggs, the dustman down the road, then he will be deemed mad and put away. Durkheim called the condition of homelessness 'anomie', meaning the lack of a nomos (Gk: law, custom or regulation), and he stressed that anomie is a feature of the social structure (or rather of a lack of social structure) before it is an individually experienced problem, and that the only effective solutions to it are social[21]. The sacred is society's solution to the problem of anomie; the sacred provides a new home world, a new security, and new meaning to life.

Man and nature

An essential ingredient in feeling at home in the world is to know what one's relation is to the non-human world, to what we call nature. There is a basic paradox in human experience here. On the one hand we know we can overcome nature; from earliest times, man has been able to control nature by means of fire, tools, domesticated animals, growing crops, and so on. But on the other hand, man has been mercilessly subject to the laws and fickleness of nature: ultimately death and sickness prove us to be part of nature. Telling man how to relate to the other inhabitants of the world and to the earth itself is one of the time-honoured functions of religion. Through ancestor cults, pantheism, creation myths and so on, man is placed in relation to the rest of the world[22].

The problem remains. For all our achievements in mastering nature through technology, we still experience starvation and illness; and as raw materials and energy threaten to run out, as pollution begins to clog up the ecosphere, and as health services prove inadequate, we are beginning to doubt our mastery over nature at the very moment of our greatest technological successes.

The technological whizz-kids claim to be the masters of nature, but their very science presupposes the laws of nature to be universal, immutable and binding on man. The ecofreaks claim us to be one with nature, yet their utopias imply a truly Promethean knowledge and mastery of nature. Neither can escape the paradox; but each tries to deny it, setting up new sacreds and new myths – progress and science on the one hand, Nature and ecology on the other – which claim to finally resolve the paradox.

Mortality

The final aspect of the human condition that the sacred addresses itself to is the universal experience of suffering, death and undeserved pain and evil. By providing something to live for, either in this world or the next, by locating ultimate reality somewhere beyond that of individual experience, the sacred provides *theodicies* that give a meaning and purpose to pain, death and injustice. A classic theodicy of times past is expressed in the well known words of the hymn:

'The rich man in his castle,
 The poor man at his gate,

God made them high and lowly
 And ordered their estate.'

This purported to justify the suffering of both landless labourer and urban proletariat and, in so far as it was believed, thereby marginally relieved their sufferings.

However objectionable we may find the ideology expressed in this hymn of a past era, it is uncertain that modern democracies have replaced it with anything else of comparable comfort to the poor, the sick and the imprisoned. Suffering today often has a peculiarly modern sting because it has neither rhyme nor reason. Perhaps one reason that America lost the Vietnam War was that it ran out of beliefs sufficiently sacred for its sons to suffer and die.

Whereas modern sacreds stoically cover up man's homelessness and try to resolve our relation to nature, they seem curiously ineffective in enabling us to come to terms with death. Indeed, this traditional function has been largely abdicated by the new sacreds, and there is now a taboo on talking about death. We treat death much as the Victorians treated sex, as something we know happens but pretend doesn't. There are as many prudish euphemisms in the way we talk about death as there were in the way Victorians alluded to sex[23]. Death is taboo because it threatens the norm that we should all be happy (part of the idol of Progress); in our culture we are not allowed to be sad, bored or in despair, or at least not to show it, and since death is the biggest single cause of sadness and despair it must be outlawed[24].

All this does not mean that death is not important, for Freud was right: the existence of a taboo indicates the repression of something crucial. There would be little need for such prohibitive norms were the prohibited subject simply to go away if ignored. Just as Freud saw sex, the taboo of the nineteeth century, as the key to unlocking the nineteenth century personality, so it may be that death, the taboo of the twentieth, is a key to understanding modern society.

Modern society has tried to abolish death, not only in talk but also in reality, and it certainly has hidden it from sight. The big reduction in infant mortality in this century is crucial here; a hundred years ago, death was a common occurrence in the family and children grew up with it, whereas today one can easily survive into middle age without having a close relative die. And even when people do die, they are likely to do so in hospital, out of sight and consequently to a degree out of mind. We now almost expect it as a human right that in an advanced technological society we should be able to live out our threescore years and ten.

This repression and invisibility of death together with the lack of theodicies creates at best uncertainty about how to cope with death when it does strike and at worst a fear of death (although note it is not *my* death which is most feared, but that of my loved ones). Inevitably, people still do die before their time, but we now feel this to be unnatural and unfair. Whereas once the death of a child was the most common kind of death, now it is the very symbol of tragedy. Further, although medicine is supposed to have postponed death and certainly has controlled some major endemic diseases, the hospitalised and medicated dying man has less control over the death-bed scene than ever before. Modern ideology holds that the individual must take control of his own destiny, yet control of the final destiny of death is denied him. Death today is still unpredictable, striking like the plague: where it will and without discrimination. The car crash, the heart attack, cancer, nuclear holocaust perhaps, may be waiting around the corner.

As Freud knew well, you cannot repress something for ever. Banished from society's respectable parlour, death has re-entered by the cultural backdoor in what Geoffrey Gorer has called the pornography of death – the portrayal of violence in the mass media, accompanied by both manifest enjoyment by the viewer and self-righteous condemnation by the guardians of morality. Violence on the screen provides a way in which death, and especially violent and unexpected death, can enter the cultural scene and be recognised, experienced and talked about by both voyeur and moralist. Even the news is obsessed with violent and unexpected death; events like car crashes, air crashes and mining disasters gain extensive coverage, not least because they are the kind of death that could have happened to you or me or our loved ones any day. Modern sacreds such as the family, the individual, science and progress fail to provide resources for coping with death, but this classic religious problem remains and accounts for much of contemporary culture.

The sacred, past and present

To sum up, modern society is uniquely in need of the sacred and is, in fact, busily repairing and revamping sacreds from the Renaissance and the Enlightenment, and from the eras of capitalism and colonialism.

Although the problems of homelessness, mortality and the relation to nature are particularly acute today, it cannot be stressed enough that these are not only modern problems but are universal human problems. Traditional society offered solutions to these problems (although from the Judaic-Christian standpoint these solutions were false); what causes trouble for modern man is the breakdown of the old solutions. But this provides us with a unique opportunity since the meaning of existence becomes problematic again and the fundamental frailty of the human condition is laid bare and can be clearly seen. From the Judaic-Christian view, then, the smashing by industrialisation and urbanisation of the once secure sacreds of traditional society is to be welcomed; their replacement by new sacreds is to be resisted.

Outline of the Book

The aim is simply to *illustrate* that modern society centres around the sacred, not to produce a *definitive* list of the top ten idols of the age. The method will be to look at various aspects of modern society in order to see whether they demonstrate the presence of the sacred.

First will be examined two social institutions, work (ch. 2) and the family (ch. 3); then a dominant form of the humanly constructed environment, suburbia (ch. 4); then a particular guiding philosophy of modern society, individualism, along with the undercurrents of collectivism (ch. 5); then will follow an analysis of a contemporary social movement, the ecology movement (ch. 6); then what may perhaps be called a social mood, racism (ch. 7); then the mass media and their role in sustaining our sense of reality and security (ch. 8); then the relation of the institutional church and contemporary theology to society (ch. 9). Social conflict and social change will be explored all too briefly in ch. 10, and the final chapter (ch. 11) will re-examine the subject of the book within an explicitly Christian framework.

It is obvious from this list that there are glaring omissions. Among social institutions education is omitted, nor is there any treatment of industry or political institutions; the glance at surburbia is to the detriment of other human environments such as the inner city or the country; the focusing on individualism as a key contemporary popular philosophy is to the detriment of the ideologies of happiness, progress, reason, the goodness of man and science, all of which are equally important, the more so because they usually get less in the way of open debate and criticism and are the more thoroughly taken for granted; for a social movement, feminism or any of the other liberation movements could have been selected; and there are other functions of the media that could have been discussed. All these omissions are justified because the aim is simply to suggest what a Christian-sociological view of society could look like, not to provide a comprehensive textbook on modern society.

Throughout, society will be described as it *is*, an essential preliminary to knowing how to change it into what it ought to be. Christians, in particular, are prone to recommending moral and political utopias without first analysing the present situation. Sociologists in general are not guilty of this, but they do make a mistake in believing that descriptive knowledge of society can be religiously neutral.

In so far as society is divided along class lines, the book is more about middle-class than working-class culture. I have drawn on my own experience in gathering much of the material, and as I am a child of the suburban middle-class this material tends to be about middle-class life. It may therefore be a happy coincidence that most readers probably will be also middle-class in origin or will be on their way into the middle-class by means of further education or a professional career, and so hopefully the book will help them interpret the culture of which they are a part. There is also a need to understand how the other half of society lives, indeed how the other half of the world lives, but that is another project.

2
Danger – Men at Work

The Problem of Work

In the middle ages, work was experienced very differently from today. In the first place, the person usually had considerable personal control over his work, at least on a day-to-day basis. The serf was a subsistence farmer involved in the whole production process from sowing through to harvesting, and he was himself the chief consumer of the crop. Likewise the craftsman in the towns organised the buying of his raw materials, worked them into the finished product, and then did the marketing and selling himself. His wife and family would participate in all this, as would any apprentices. People identified with their work; this is shown in medieval art and icons, in which people chose to be portrayed and remembered at work, whereas in western art today workscenes are virtually absent.

Secondly, work gave the person an assured place in society. Medieval society was not composed of modern social *classes* allowing movement up or down the social scale, but of *estates* into which one was born and in which one normally had to stay for life. Once a noble, always a noble; once a serf, always a serf. This meant that to be a serf, or an urban tradesman, immediately placed you firmly in the social hierarchy – contrast today when to be a student or a shorthand typist indicates rather less about where in the social scale you have come from and what your life chances are. Being a serf may not have been very wonderful in lots of ways – one was on perpetual call-up for military service to one's local lord, one had to turn over a tithe to the church, and in the modern sense of civil liberties one was totally unfree. But it did tell you who you were, it gave you a place in the world (even if not a very prestigious place), and it gave you considerable control over your daily labour.

Some time after the break-up of feudal society, a new approach to work emerged in several northern European countries, an approach which usually goes under the name of the Protestant ethic[1]. This broke with the medieval Catholic worldview which put 'nature' or 'the world' in an inferior position to 'grace' and which saw secular work as inferior to the religious life of prayer and worship. By contrast, the puritans saw the world as the arena into which God had called them, and work was a crucial part of that calling. In its theological form, this approach saw work as a response to being saved, but in circles which believed strongly in predestination there was the problem of knowing whether or not one's name was in the book of life, and so hard work and financial success became a sign that one was indeed saved. Either way, work was a religious calling. It is not surprising that this religious view of work took strong hold on pioneer settler communities such as New England and South Africa in the seventeenth century, for it provided the motivation necessary to keep at the hard labour of clearing the virgin wilderness into fields and setting up towns and communities.

However, the very effectiveness of this view of work in promoting economic development meant that it could be easily de-Christianised; that is, work became seen as a good thing in its own right – its being a Christian calling becoming simply a veneer and then later being dropped altogether. Work itself became an honourable thing, irrespective of one's religious beliefs. As such it became a powerful ideology for the masters of the early industrial revolution. Their problem was how to get their new labour force to accommodate itself to the machine[2] – the subsistence peasant or rural labourer had been used to working flexibly as the weather and the seasons dictated, and was also accustomed to an enormous number of religious feast days and holidays. But in the modern factory it became necessary for workers to turn up at a fixed time every day of the week and to keep at it until the hooter went at the end of the day. Wholly new concepts of time and of responsibility to the master and to the machine were necessary. Without the day-to-day contact with the master craftsman or the tenant farmer that the apprentice or labourer enjoyed, the new industrial worker needed internal motivation to keep him at his increasingly soul-less labour. The idea that work was itself an honourable thing provided just such a motivation, and the coinciding of this work ethic with other circumstances enabled the economic take-off that we call the industrial revolution.

The heyday of this ethic was the nineteenth century. For those who grasped the opportunities for social and economic advancement that nineteenth century commerce offered, work became the chief means to that end, and the idea that work could be an end in itself was immensely appealing. Work became the central and therefore sacred value in terms of which a man's worth was measured. The priests who maintained the shrine of work were the middle classes, and they wasted no time in bringing the labouring classes to worship at the shrine. In particular the Poor Law expressed the belief that the most heinous sin was not to be willing to work, or not to work as hard as one was able.

Even Karl Marx was typical of his century when he developed an economic and social theory based on the assumption that productive activity is man's central defining characteristic and that fulfilment at work is the key to human happiness. (It is no coincidence that some communist regimes today appear somewhat puritanical in their attitudes to work.) And we have inherited a not dissimilar view that the economy is all important. In Britain interminable moans are heard in the media that the country is declining, and these moans are based not so much on the country's diminishing military capability or on the end of Empire but on poor economic performance. Because Britain is steadily moving down the European economic league table, it is believed that the country as a whole and in every department is in a mess. Moral calls by church leaders seem to be similarly sparked off by the economic rather than by the moral state of the nation. The world over, governments rise and fall chiefly over their handling of the economy. Work, productivity, and the economy are seen as the measure of a nation, and it takes a war (e.g. World War II, Vietnam, or the guerrilla war in Zimbabwe) for other criteria such as freedom, liberation, or democracy, to rise to the surface as alternative values which might be a better measure of a nation.

So we have arrived at a world in which work is idolised in the sense that economic performance is seen as an important measure of the worth of an individual and as *the* measure of the worth of a society. But alongside this elevation of work and economics there are some rather unfortunate features of work. The division of labour has meant that we, unlike the subsistence peasant or the traditional craftsman, do not see the whole production process through from beginning to end, and our only objective reward at the end of the day is the wage packet. Nor are we in control of the conditions of work. Even professional people like doctors and social workers, who would like to feel they had escaped this kind of alienation, find their work involves processing 'cases' in much the same way that the factory worker processes materials: a case is handed on to the professional from another agency in the health or welfare system, the professional then performs some fairly specialist and technical operation on the case, which he then hands on to be processed further down the line by some other agency. He is no more likely to see the product of his labours than the car worker is to see the finished car.

Furthermore, decisions at work are taken away from the shopfloor; even in medicine, major decisions are taken not in the operating theatre or in the ward but by the hospital administrators or by a regional health board. Since decisions are taken by someone other than the worker, they are based on criteria which are at best unknown to the worker and at worst foreign to his interests. This means that decisions often appear to him as wrong, stupid, or arbitrary. During an era of economic cuts such as the 1970s, this has become one of the attractions of self-employment; even though his budget may be comparatively small, the self-employed person can determine his own priorities and order the resources he needs. But the teacher, social worker, hospital doctor, or university lecturer finds that economy measures are taken by administrators with different priorities, so that although the expenditure per man may still be relatively high the individual worker finds himself lacking what he sees as essential resources.

A further feature of work today is its mediocrity. In previous eras, there was much work that was inherently satisfying, such as that of the traditional craftsman, and there was much work that was really terrible, such as that performed by slaves. But at each of these extremes man had a place in the world, and knew who he was. Now, by contrast, we have eliminated the worst forms of utterly degrading work, but at the same time we have professionalised and bureaucratised the more creative occupations and enmeshed the self-employed in a web of equally alienating fiscal and legal regulations. Work is in general safe, not unpleasant and not unsatisfying, but it is not something to shout about.

All this has produced a peculiarly modern problem at work. On the one hand we retain elements of the view of work as a calling which we expect *should* be meaningful and fulfilling, yet the organisation of work in modern industrial society is such that it does not fulfil this expectation[3]. We have created the ideology that a person's worth depends on his work, but then we so structure things that work is singularly mediocre. In other words, we persuade people that work is a god to be worshipped, and then do not provide altars at which they may worship this god.

In such a situation, people do their utmost to persuade themselves that their work *is* meaningful in one way or another. Umpteen studies have shown that, surprisingly, people are on the whole satisfied with their work, and claim not to be alienated. As one author puts the problem:

> 'What is alarming is not that we have a high degree of "alienation" (we don't), but that so many people invest meaningless activity with meaning, trivial work with high significance.'[4]

And Peter Berger has commented that what unites the executive and the janitor is that for both of them their work consists of pretending to be what they are not. How do they manage it? How do we all manage it? This is a central question for the sociology of work. In general, there are three ways – seeing work as expressive, as instrumental, and in terms of human relations. Let's look at each of these in turn.

The Meaning of Work

Some people manage to see work as *expressive*, as an expression of their own talents, creativity, or individuality. They do not work primarily in order to earn a living, rather they live in order to work; their work is their life. A classic example is the artist who has resisted pressures to commercialise his work; he espouses the view introduced by the romantic movement of the eighteenth and nineteenth centuries that art is the personal expression of the individual, and if he is lucky he will find people prepared to pay him and grant him high esteem for his personal expressions. More likely he will remain unlucky and poor.

More fortunate in regard to status and remuneration are expressive workers such as doctors, architects, and engineers who feel that, although they may not be particularly creative or personal in their work, they are at least using their personal talents. But as already mentioned, they are subject to bureaucratic control and, as has been shown by recent wage demands by professionals such as doctors, nurses, and university lecturers, there is also a large instrumental element in their approach to work.

The *instrumental* work ethic sees the purpose of work to be the earning of a wage or salary, and is by far the most widespread view of work in contemporary society. This view is taken for granted in all kinds of ways: conventional economics sees the prime purpose of industry as making a profit and the prime intention of the worker as selling his labour for the highest price, other motivations being seen as secondary, 'uneconomic' or irrational. In Britain, the tax system is criticised by politicians, economists and laymen, because 'it doesn't make it worth working', both at the top of the supertax bracket where it is not worth putting in extra work because it is virtually all taxed away, and in the poverty trap at the bottom where an extra pound of earnings leads to the loss of slightly over a pound of welfare benefits and allowances. These complaints assume that the chief reason that people work is that they want the money.

Indeed, work is even *defined* in these terms, as activity which is paid. Thus every week in Britain when over a million unemployed sign on they are confronted at the counter by a prominent sign which says, 'Before claiming, please tell the clerk if you have done any work since last claiming benefit'; what this sign means is, please tell the clerk if you have received any income from any time spent in the previous week. If, for example, I were to declare at the counter that in the last week I had written this chapter (what I myself call work) or had decorated my home, this would be followed by a rather protracted and muddled conversation between myself and the clerk, at the end of which he would ascertain that I had not been paid for this activity – so why had I wasted their time telling them about it?

There is no clear relation between productive activity and the conventional definition of work. An overmanned job in which one is working below capacity or in which most of the time is spent drinking tea or coffee is defined as work. Spending a weekend decorating one's house is not defined as work because it is not paid, whereas exactly the same task carried out by a painter and decorator is defined as work. It is on this basis that the number of people employed is calculated (the most obvious and glaring absurdity in this definition being the omission of housework as work); similarly, unemployment statistics are based on a definition of unemployment not as not doing anything, but as not being paid while wanting to be paid. The division of time into 'work' which is part of the productive economy, and 'leisure' which is part of consumption, is based on this instrumental view of work, that work is what one is paid for. Since the whole of economics and the social security system are based on this idea, it is rather hard to avoid it even if one tries; in short, the instrumental view of work is the chief way in which our society infuses meaning into work.

For the individual the meaning of work is found outside work. This is not to say that work is unimportant, but that it is important not as an end in itself but as a means to other valued ends. The most common of these is the family, and men especially see their work as the way in which they provide for their family. For others, the wage packet is what enables them to have a good time, while for yet others such as the teenager, the housewife or the poor, work may be seen as the means to freedom and the path out of economic dependence on parents, husband, or welfare handouts.

The fact that the meaning of work is found outside work does not mean that work is not important for the individual. Its sacramental importance can be of at least three kinds. First, for men especially, it is central to their self-concept and self-esteem. Their sense of manliness may be bound up with the idea of the male being the stronger of the sexes who goes out and provides for wife and children. The fact that the job itself may be dangerous, boring or otherwise unattractive may become a positive asset, for the nastier the job the more the man's sticking to it declares his love for family. Thus to become unemployed can be a great blow to a man; it is not just the loss of earning power, but also the concept of being a man that is attacked. Even though being made redundant is manifestly the result of economic forces beyond the individual worker's control, he experiences it as a personal attack. In general, women do not find redundancy attacks their sexuality and identity in the same way, for they are more likely to see going to work in expressive terms, or for the little extras that the money can buy, or for the sociability it provides. In an age of inequality, their problem is getting a good job in the first place, not getting sacked later on.

However, there are indications that many middle class women do go into paid employment for reasons of self-esteem and personal liberation. Much of the voluntary and philanthropic work that occupied their forebears has now been professionalised (e.g. social work, nursing) and what voluntary organisations remain do so only by courtesy of the professions which limit the scope for innovative or creative work within the voluntary organisations. (The term 'voluntary' to denote organised but unpaid labour itself indicates that ordinarily work is done of necessity in order to earn money.) David Riesman comments[5]:

> 'Reacting to this situation, the women either sink back into indifference or conclude, like their working class sisters, that only through a job, a culturally defined job (i.e. a paid job), will they be liberated. Instead of moving toward autonomy in play, an autonomy toward which they could also help their men, they often simply add to their own domestic problems all the anxieties men endure at work.'

If work (= a paid job) is crucial to the unliberated man's concept of himself as breadwinner of the family, it is also becoming crucial in much the same way to the so-called liberated woman's concept of herself as liberated and autonomous. The ethic that work = worth is a thread running from seventeenth century puritanism to twentieth century feminism.

Secondly, work provides status and esteem not only in the eyes of the individual but also in the eyes of others. Although one's occupation does not define one's status with quite the same stability and exactitude that being an earl or a serf did in medieval times, nevertheless occupation is still one of the most important ways in which we compare ourselves with others and are compared by them. In settings where one cannot readily be identified in terms of who one knows or who one is related to, the most common introductory question on being introduced to someone is, 'What's your job?' – for this is the single question that is most likely to give us an indication of the sort of person he is, his interests, and how the conversation should proceed. That one person is a dustman and another a neuro-surgeon tells us quite a lot about him, rightly or wrongly.

But it is not just on being introduced to each other that

people see work as the provider of status. In Britain, the Registrar General, when compiling the Census and other statistics based on it, uses occupation to determine the social class of each person. Those with a professional job are listed in social class I, and so on all the way through to the unskilled worker in social class V, and within each class subdivisions are also based on occupation.

Thirdly, our work 'places' us in the economic as well as in the social hierarchy, for it is our wage packet or salary that determines our purchasing power. This is perhaps an especially important reason why married women who have not been trained for a career go out to work, for it reduces their economic dependence on the husband and relocates them in the power structure of both marriage and society as a whole.

It is important to note that even if the individual does not perceive his work to be central in his life, it still *is* central, whether he likes it or not. Work *does* place him in the social and economic hierarchies, and whether he likes it or not, money and status *are* important means by which other people place him. This is a good example of how difficult it is to declare unilateral independence from the sacred: even if a person does not consciously make work central to his life, it is still central.

It is quite an achievement on the part of society that each of the three ways in which work is instrumentally important – self-esteem, status, and economic purchasing power – may still be experienced by the individual even though his work is itself boring, dangerous, unhealthy, or socially destructive. By locating the meaning of work in factors extrinsic to work itself we have solved our historically induced need to find meaning in work that is generally rather mundane.

We have solved the problem by positively embracing alienation; we work not for anything inherent in the work itself but for reasons alien to the work itself. We have solved the problem of the mundaneness of work by reducing the importance of the work process and focusing the worker's eyes elsewhere, on the remuneration and status associated with his work. So there is in general rather less enthusiasm than might be expected on the part of workers for proposals for worker involvement in management; such schemes point to the worker's lack of control over his work and suggest that industrial relations would be improved if a measure of control were restored to him, but until the worker becomes committed to the work *process*, such proposals are unlikely to be successful.

In addition to the expressive and instrumental meanings of work, there is a third way in which people find meaning at work, and this has to do with *sociability*. This is generated at work, either through directly cooperating with one's fellows, or in the breaks between work. A sense of solidarity may be engendered either through doing the same job or because of the unpleasantness of the work. In some industries such as mining and deep-sea fishing danger produces a solidarity which may be central to the man's sense of identity. Many workers though, while valuing social relations at work, rigidly separate this from their home and leisure life. Others, however, deliberately spend their leisure time with their workmates; miners are one example (although in a mining community they may have little choice), and professional people often use work as a source of contacts for meeting people on a social level.

This aspect of work may be taken for granted by many workers. The housewife, though, isolated at home, may develop an image of paid employment as highly sociable and may go out to work for precisely this reason. For those who have worked all their lives, however, the sociability of work is more a pleasant by-product than the reason for going to work. Sociability usually becomes a motive only when one misses it, and here lies one root of the problems that many men have on retirement. For the first time in their adult life, they are confronted with a drastically reduced social circle, and marital tensions may develop that had lain dormant for those years when one or both partners related to others outside the marriage.

Social relations at work are closely related to the simple experience of being occupied in a daily round that is part social, part practical. At the very least, this round fills up the day, and for the person who relies heavily on work to provide this the weekend can be devastatingly empty. A psychiatrist describes this as follows:

> 'The real emptiness and ultimate poverty of meaning of his existence comes to the fore as soon as his vocational activity is halted for a certain period: on Sundays. In any city, Sunday is the saddest day of the week. It is on Sunday, when the tempo of the working week is suspended, that the poverty of meaning in everyday urban life is exposed.'[6]

These three meanings of work – expressive, instrumental, and social – are not mutually exclusive. There may well be an element of all three in the work of any one individual. They are presented here as what sociologists call 'ideal types', by which is meant not desirable types but characterisations that, while perhaps not fitting perfectly any one individual or society, nevertheless illuminate aspects of social reality.

The power of these three meanings of work is perhaps best seen when people are denied work and in the problems experienced in redundancy, retirement and Sunday. Of these, long-term unemployment is probably the most detrimental to the individual psyche. While retirement is something that it is possible to prepare for, and Sunday is something that has a foreseeable end (however interminable some Sundays may seem), involuntary redundancy followed by long-term unemployment comes with little warning and increasingly appears to the individual to have no end. He may feel his talents being wasted, lose self-respect and standing in the community, descend to the poverty line, and find the daytime appallingly empty. But perhaps surprisingly, even the person who no longer has a family to provide for, and who did not value work particularly for its status, sociability or income, often finds unemployment harrowing and would rather be in work; which indicates how sacred work is. It is when we find a situation in which people feel utterly lost and dejected that we are on the right trail in the search for idols. Once we can identify what people are missing in such a situation, then it is highly likely that that element is an idol. People's experience of redundancy, retirement, and Sunday all point to work being a sacrament which people cannot do without.

The Future of Work

If the ideology that work = worth has been so long-lived, and over three centuries has succeeded in mobilising nations into economic expansion and providing many people with a sense of worth, how well will this ideology serve the economy and the individual in the foreseeable future? Forecasting the future is an uncertain business (and ideologically tinged, in that each scenario of the future tends to justify the interests and values of a particular group of people), but one prediction that has some plausibility is that of mass unemployment due to automation. Of course, there have been fears of technologically induced unemployment since the beginning of the industrial revolution and, although often justified in the short term in that people were indeed thrown out of work by new machinery, mechanisation has not yet been the cause of long-term structural unemployment. But there is no reason why the replacement of brain-power by computerisation need follow the pattern of the replacement of muscle-power by mechanisation; the mechanisation of agriculture and industry was accompanied by a vast expansion in employment in the service sector of the economy, but it is precisely in this service sector that automation promises (or threatens) to make the deepest inroads.

If the idolising of work while the actual nature of work became more and more mundane produced the problem of the meaning of work, then the continuing idolising of the work ethic combined with mass unemployment is likely to create an even greater problem. It may be possible to find ways of conning ourselves that mundane work is worthwhile but, so long as we believe in the work ethic, it is hard to see how we can con ourselves that not to work is worthwhile. And study both of history and of the present suggests that the work ethic shows no signs of losing popularity; the hysteria shown by some people about social security scroungers, together with the tiny number of such scroungers, suggest that the work ethic is alive and well. The future then may hold a store of trouble, for, if we say that a man's (and now also a woman's) worth is based on work, yet as a society we fail to provide work for all but a small minority, then there can be little doubt that the one occupation which *will* be well manned in future is psychiatry.

Not that the past has been all that rosy. To say that a man's worth is based on what he does, like any status system based on *achievement*, leads to the problem that we cannot all be winners. A proportion of the population is bound to achieve less than others and so be assigned a place at the bottom of the pile. The other way of assigning social and personal worth is for it to be *ascribed* to the individual by birth. In a large family, for example, although there may be some rivalry between children, if the parents value each child simply because he is alive then it is possible for each child to feel he is uniquely important. But on the scale of a whole society, ascribing worth equally and fully to every member simply by virtue of his membership of that society has never worked and seems utterly utopian. In practice, ascriptive status systems have given social worth only to a small minority (usually those in power) and have functioned to keep the majority in a subject position. This was the negative side of the feudal society mentioned earlier, for, although everyone had a place and this led to a sense of security, most people's place was an inferior one. Socially, people felt secure, but inferior.

It is instructive here to take a second look at the Protestant ethic. In its practical form, it meant that people worked hard in order to assure and validate their salvation; but in the theology of early Protestant reformers such as Luther, work was not a means to salvation but the free and grateful response to salvation. That is to say, one's worth was assured by God, and one then worked in the world on the basis of that worth. Work was a response to being valued, rather than a means to being valued. Curiously, there is some affinity here with the aristocratic concept of work not as a means to achieving social worth, for that was ascribed to one by birth, but as a response to that privilege. For the aristocrat, work was done out of freedom not necessity (which is why it is today unaristocratic and a cause for complaint by the landed gentry that they often *have* to work in order to maintain their stately homes).

If we could rediscover the idea of work as a free response to our being valued rather than as a necessity in order that we may be valued, we would be well on the way both to a concept of work that is more in line with the biblical view of the free person, and to solving the trouble ahead in an automated future. The next few paragraphs will explore some of the practical implications of work as a response to being valued rather than as a means to being valued. If work, along with other things, can become a response to *already* having personal and social worth, then unemployment loses many of its terrors; for if paid employment is not available as a means of expressing the joy of being alive, then other means surely will be available. But this requires *a*) a society in which *all* people are valued irrespective of their achievements, and *b*) there is some means for distributing the wealth produced by the few to all members of society. Although these appear sizeable demands, steps have already been taken along both these lines.

Firstly, the universalising of ascriptive value – the creation of a society in which each member feels worthwhile simply by being a member of that society. If we compare our own society either with Victorian society or with many societies today which do not enjoy civil and political liberties, it becomes apparent that simply by being born into a modern democracy the individual is valued as a free person whose freedom is to be protected and as a rational person whose rationality is allowed expression in the ballot box. Although freedom and rationality can be denied in certain circumstances such as committal to prison or mental hospital, they cannot be removed simply because one is not as gifted and does not achieve as much in this world as the next person.

This view of civil and political rights could be extended

into a concept of economic rights, that is, every person has a right to an adequate income simply by virtue of being a member of an advanced industrial society. Now one might think that this has already been embodied in the Welfare State as envisaged by Lord Beveridge in the 1940s, but this is not so. Access to unemployment and supplementary benefits is not granted simply because one belongs to society; it is granted only so long as the recipient shows signs of the work ethic, continues to try to find paid employment and repents for having failed. As the leaflet 'Responsibilities of Claimants', that is handed to all those claiming unemployment and supplementary benefits in Britain, says:

> 'You must not sign the declaration on your claim form unless you are and were for any day covered by the claim prepared to accept at once any offer of employment suitable in your case. . . .'

The social security system merely makes a minor concession to the dominant ideology that a person is worth something only if he works, by adding that he may also be deemed worthy if he *wants* to work. Work is still sacred, and kept firmly in the realm of necessity rather than the realm of freedom.

Some critics, therefore, advocate a guaranteed subsistence income accorded all members of society[7]. In addition, those wishing and able to find paid employment would receive an additional income from their employer, and people would also be free to become self-employed and earn a supplementary income from their own businesses. Such a system would remove the stigma presently attaching to the unemployed, and would restore them to being full members of the community. The present system in a very real way denies them what is supposedly an inalienable right in a free society. In theological terms, this would be an economy based on grace rather than works, inclusion by right rather than exclusion until proved worthy[7].

The transfer of work from the realm of necessity into that of freedom (which automation would make possible, if only we were to abandon the work ethic) would provide a degree of flexibility which is presently unknown. As one advocate of the guaranteed income writes of the American scene (and much the same applies in Britain), it would largely break down the present dichotomy between 'straight' society and the so-called 'counter culture':

> 'Young people growing up in today's world are faced with what could be called economic tyranny. Well-paying jobs in large organisations are available, complete with all the elements generally referred to as the rat race. Other than something like the Peace Corps, however, there are few other alternatives except dropping out completely . . . At present, there is very little middle ground; for the most part, you are either in the system or out of it, and for many individuals neither alternative is very satisfying. The guaranteed income would offer a major new alternative.'[8]

But who is going to pay for all this? It seems clear that it would only work in a prosperous, automated society, and there is a problem here because, while a guaranteed income system would be most easily set up in a time of economic buoyancy, it would be most needed in a time of recession and high unemployment. But it would not cost that much more than the present social security system, and it should be seen in the context of the historical progression toward re-organising the economies of industrial societies so that more and more people are receiving a bigger and bigger proportion of their net income from the state. Child benefits, old-age pensions, nationalised industries, subsidies, and so on mean that now it is not uncommon in industrial societies for up to 60% of a nation's wealth to be distributed through public channels. Given that the guaranteed incomes would together come to far less than 60% of the national income, the financial feasability of the guaranteed income does not seem so impossible. Administratively, such a system could be much simpler than present social security systems.

One of the most interesting moves in this direction is the Youth Opportunities Programme which operates on the belief that young people who have never succeeded in finding a job have a right not only to social security but also to work. As the Programme advertises itself to businesses:

> 'The idea is extremely simple: If you can take in young people for up to six months, we will pay them £19.50 a week.'[9]

This particular advert is permeated with the work ethic in that it believes that without paid employment young people will come to see themselves as 'dustbin kids' of no worth, and on this ideological level the advert is damaging. But it does embody a fiscal principle which is promisingly radical in that work is provided on the basis of a guaranteed income from society, rather than income being earned on the basis of work. Since ideologies often change to accommodate themselves to economic practices that have grown to be the norm over time, in the long term the economic principle of the Youth Opportunities Programme, if embodied in other programmes (and with increasing unemployment this is likely), may form fertile soil for future ideological change.

A Footnote on Materialism

Sex and money are often believed to be the idols of the age; let us look briefly at the so-called worship of money. As already mentioned, the economy is believed to be the measure of the state of a nation and in this sense the gross earning power of a nation has become pre-eminent. But a key test of whether or not something is an ultimate commitment is whether people would name it in reply to the question 'What do you live for?', and remarkably few people would claim to live for money. Yet clearly people are keen to earn money, and considerably more money than is needed for subsistence, so it is perhaps worth considering what people say about why they want money.

Firstly, money buys goods, and the goods purchased by an individual or family compose their immediate physical environment. We use goods to create an environment that is our very own, that sustains the image of ourselves that we would like, and that gives us a sense of being at home. The student may buy his stereo set and give it pride of place in his room because this declares his commitment to a certain kind of youth subculture which provides him with a sense of identity. He buys posters to pin to the wall because these mark off the room as his very own rather than as a soulless apartment like countless others provided by halls of residence or landladies. Much the same is true but on a larger scale with the young married couple furnishing their new home – carpets, curtains, paint and wallpapers all make a rather ordinary house into their very own home. They give the couple a sense of control and a feeling that they have a place in the soulless city. And so on, right up to the extremes engaged in by the aristocracy of the seventeenth and eighteenth centuries who not only furnished the interiors of their stately homes with the most expensive furniture but also landscaped the view as far as the eye could see from the house; all this gave the feeling of being in control and of having a place in the world. In brief, goods create homes[10]. Chapter one indicated the religious nature of this need for home, for a place in the universe. Ultimately, people say they need money to attain security, for themselves and their family. If there is an idol here, it is not money but security; a secure sense of place in the order of things.

Goods are used not only to create an environment, but also as aids to identity. The well-cut suit may be crucial to a man's sense of respectability and reliability at work and in public gatherings. The multi-billion dollar cosmetics industry is geared toward promoting goods which confirm a woman's sense of her own feminity, while the motor industry promotes aids to masculinity. Status symbols proclaim one's aspirations: conspicuous consumption is indulged in not so much so that others can see how well-off one is but so that they can see how refined one's taste is, how modern and avante-garde one is, or how one values the traditional virtues embodied in reproduction antique furniture.

A related use of goods is their ability to buy their owner into a social group. The system of buying rounds in a bar symbolises a sense of solidarity and oneness with the group, and continued participation in this ritual system of exchange may be necessary if one is to continue to be part of the group. Similarly, the paraphernalia of the youth culture (from skateboards to fashion shoes) represents the teenager's membership of the group and his or her disidentification from the status of child. Much of the specialist ware of various sports is not strictly essential for the successful pursuance of the sport, but is important for representing oneself as a fully-fledged member of the sporting group.

As with goods that organise our *physical* environment, those goods that provide identity and an entrée to a group provide us with control over our *social* environment; they provide us with the place in society that we desire. The ultimate end is not the money, nor the goods it buys, but a place in the societal sun and a sense of self-respect. The root of this need appears to be in the fundamental homelessness of mankind.

'Simple living', cutting down on an individual's standard of living, has become the vogue in certain circles. But unless this movement understands the root causes of materialism, then its efforts will be largely in vain. Until people feel secure, until they have a place in the order of things that is inviolable, then their motivation to acquire and accumulate and furnish their nest will remain undiminished. Only when we resolve the human problem of ultimate homelessness can the impulse to acquire and to furnish be voluntarily relinquished. Indeed, for many people the 'simple living' movement may be yet another way of trying to create an artificial sense of security. Having been made conscious that their previous place in the world was dependent on the poverty of the Third World, they find their consciences cannot live with this knowledge. Their sense of place has been undermined by their consciences, and subsequent attempts to 'live more simply that others might live' (the motto of the lifestyle movement) become attempts to salve their consciences and thereby restore the sense of occupying a valid moral place in the world.

The second reason that people give for needing money is that they want to *preserve* their standard of living. This motive is barely different from those already mentioned. In a time of inflation, there is the problem not only of making a place for oneself in the world, but also of maintaining that place. This too derives from the need for security.

Many people need money to buy desired goods, while the teenager and the woman in the process of liberating herself may need it to buy freedom. But far and away the most common need is to provide for the family – the husband believes he needs to earn in order to provide for his wife, and his wife believes she needs the housekeeping in order to provide for the children. It is the idolising of the family which keeps our economic system and our materialism going, and that keeps up the desire to earn. Perhaps this is one factor leading to the generally more conservative political hue of women, for they do not cherish the possibility of economic uncertainty and reduced family income that may accompany the political struggle for radical change. It is the concern for families that has broken many a strike; a man dare not fail to provide for wife and children.

The prime importance of parents providing for their own children is embodied in the British welfare system. All kinds of inadequate parental care will go unheeded by welfare agencies (so long as the child does not get into trouble with the police); similarly, there may be violence between the marital partners but the welfare state will not intervene (so long as the violated partner does not complain); baby battering may go unnoticed. In general the welfare state is reluctant to intervene in the privacy of a family. A couple, if they can afford it, can totally abandon responsibility for the day-to-day care of their children by employing nannies or packing the children off to boarding school. But the one form of family neglect which *will* lead to intervention by social workers is if the parents find themselves unable to provide for their children and request financial support (additional to social security) from the state. In such circumstances, social workers assume that it is not the finances but the parents that are inadequate. In our society, to be deemed an adequate parent you can do virtually anything in your family so long as you keep it quiet, but the one thing you must not do is fail to support it financially. Ask any father-in-law.[11]

The belief in the family as the pre-eminent value which justifies the earning and spending of money has been grossly exploited by advertisers. They know that one of the best ways to sell a product is to convince people that it is essential for the health, happiness or security of their family. Thus, your husband will love you if you buy him a certain after-shave, your children will grow up healthy if you buy a certain breakfast cereal or a certain disinfectant, your family can smile through adversity only if you buy life insurance, your children will get a good start in life only if you buy them a children's encyclopaedia or a private education, and so on *ad nauseam*. If there is one thing that fuels the fires of materialism in the West it is love of the family. To identify materialism as the idol may miss the root causes of materialism, and one of these is the idolising of the family. This is the subject of the next chapter.

3
The Do-It-Yourself Family

Having identified money and sex as modern idols, moralists often then proceed to set against them 'good' things such as work and the family. Recent calls for the upholding of family life and laments over the present state of the family by moral entrepreneurs such as the Festival of Light indicate the family to be the last thing one would suspect society of idolising.

This chapter queries this. It has already been argued that the family gives meaning to work, but it will be suggested now that the family is an even more pervasive provider of meaning and, far from being 'in decline', is seen as sacred in modern society. The more important a social institution, the more likely it is to become a source of meaning and an object of worship.

Privatisation

In modern societies, most people do not feel involved in politics and economics, in the public arenas of life. Most are content to vote once every four or five years, but have no great illusions about their ability to really change the face of the country. Involvement in local politics is minimal; relatively few workers are actively involved in their trade union; and few shareholders attend annual general meetings. We are content, or resigned, to let someone else run the show. Similarly, although lip service is paid to the benefits that science and technology can confer, few understand let alone have any control over these leviathans; instead we are resigned to accepting the words and figures of the technical experts.

Even those aspects of the public sphere which are supposedly oriented to the needs of the consumer can be impersonal and alienating. As consumers, we feel threatened by the impersonality and unresponsiveness of bureaucracy (the tax man, the social security, the local authority), of medicine (waiting lists, doctors who don't listen to patients), of schools (which determine the fate of our children but over which we have little control), the telly (violence and sex enter the living room and our children's minds with or without our consent), and so on.

At the same time as these larger social institutions are getting more remote from the ordinary person, there has been a decline in the importance of smaller community structures such as the trade guild, the village or the corner shop. As a result, society is now composed largely of individuals plus the ponderous giants of bureaucracy and technology, with relatively little left in between. Worse, the idea of democracy to which all pay lip service informs us that we *should* be able to influence things at the mass level, yet we know we cannot; so we feel mildly guilty about national and world events, and dissatisfied with those in charge. The feudal serf had no more control at this political level, but he did not expect to have. As with the ideology of work, so with politics, increasing expectations have not been accompanied by changes which would enable these expectations to be met. As a result, people experience a mixture of disgruntlement and apathy over politics. The individual is homeless within the mass society.

A common solution to this is what sociologists call *privatisation* – a retreat into the private area of personal life. For some people, this may involve a personal religion stressing individual salvation and a personally holy and moral life[1]. For others, privatisation could mean a retreat into hobbies or sport, but for the great majority it means a retreat into the womb of family life. It is in the family, modern people believe, that meaning, love and warmth are to be found. This is most clearly manifested in the notion of romantic love in which exclusive love between two people is seen as the highest form of human relationship. (This has not always been so. Jesus, for example, living in another era, never used marital affection as a parable for the love of God.) When the family and marriage become the focus of life and meaning in this way, they become sacred.

In traditional societies, people unthinkingly embrace the social roles they play in daily life. The tribesman identifies with his daily activities and sees himself as a hunter, father, and member of the tribe. In modern society, by contrast, we distance ourselves from our roles: we say 'It's only a role, it's not the real me.' Underneath our daily activities, we believe there is a 'real me'. My daily activities may be inherently mundane and boring, and my influence in the world at large non-existent, yet I may be able to maintain self-respect because I believe these observable actions and situations I'm routinely involved in are not the real me. (The neurotic may make a similar distinction between role and self in the opposite way. Despite manifest success in the world he may continue to believe that he himself is worthless and a failure.) Either way around, the distinction between role and self is a peculiarly modern distinction. Whereas once upon a time roles provided a person with identity, now they are believed to be a threat to identity. (The modern young person living in an archaically traditional rural community will therefore find the village's identification of himself with his roles stifling, and he may long to break from these identifying ties and move to the anonymous city where he can 'be himself'.)

But it is difficult if my image of myself is hourly contradicted by the things I do. Difficult at any rate if I try to go it alone. If only there were someone else who knew me well enough to know the real me and whose very presence constantly reinforced my sense of the real me. This is where the modern nuclear family, consisting of the nucleus of husband, wife and dependent children, comes in. This is why people talk of 'being themselves' at home. In modern society, marriage and the family enable me to construct a home world in which I am known as the self I would like to be and in which I, in turn, confirm the self of my spouse. Or at least this is the hope. Marriage and the family provide a whole universe of meanings which is for the family members real reality as opposed to the artificial reality of the public world out there[2]. Marriage provides a do-it-yourself reality kit, or, as *The Seekers* song puts it, a chance to create a 'world of our own', a world that 'no-one else can share'. Once the couple have begun to create a world of their own, starting up a family is a sure way to cement this world. The child grows up into the world of the parents' making, takes it for granted, and thereby adds another actor who confirms the reality of the whole show. This is why starting a family is often seen by people as a way of 'cementing the marriage'.

The do-it-yourself reality kit that marriage and the family provide makes them enduringly popular. As many people are getting married as ever, and those who get divorced usually remarry within a short time; even if the experience of marriage is unhappy, the *idea* of marriage is still believed in and people are willing to have another go. As with the dereliction felt by the unemployed who have relied on work for a sense of worth, so people who have been divorced may possibly find they had relied on marriage for a sense of reality and usually they just can't stand the loss of this reality. For the widowed, it may be worse; as Philippe Aries puts it in his fascinating study of western attitudes to death: 'A single person is missing for you, and the whole world is empty.' We are more fearful of the death of a loved one than of our own death[3].

But you may say, surely marriage is a basic human institution and has always been? Yet historian Philippe Aries[4] considers family life to have been held in far less esteem in the middle ages than today:

> 'True, men and women will always go on loving one another, will always go on having children. . . . It would be vain to deny the existence of a family life in the Middle Ages. But the family existed in silence: it did not awaken feelings strong enough to inspire poet or artist. . . . Not much value was placed on the family.'

Why then do so many people today believe that the family is in decline? It is because modern marriage, although inordinately popular, is also inordinately precarious.

('Modern' here means 'as opposed to pre-industrial'. People experience today's family as normal, natural and from everlasting, but in the longer time perspective of history and sociology marriage may appear to be a rather recent invention.)

For a start, the defences of the family against the outside public world may not be strong enough. The outside world enters through thin air into the living room via the telly, the radio and the papers. We are made constantly aware that other people have found a better lifestyle than us, have the perfect marriage, or have more satisfying jobs. Advertising constantly confronts us with ever higher material standards which become further and further beyond our reach. Kitchen sink dramas on the telly remind us of the cracks that could appear in our own marriage at any moment.

But the cracks may come from within the family itself. Mother-in-law may constantly be trying to disrupt the reality the couple has created for itself; adolescent children may bring home 'undesirable' friends, indulge in music the parents can't stand let alone understand, or may not fulfil the hopes the parents had of them. Whether it's mother-in-law or the rebelling teenager, the result is that the 'Englishman's castle' is taken from within. In some families, the simple fact of the eventual departure of offspring may spark a crisis if the sense of reality in the marriage had come to rely on the stabilising effect of the children; when the children leave home, the reality evaporates and the couple realise with horror that they have nothing in common.

This precariousness of marriage derives from the fact that in our culture marriage is based on love, on sex and sentiment, whereas in most traditional societies marriage is based on the exchange of property or is in some other way integrated into the community. As another historian, Edward Shorter[5], puts it:

> 'Formerly, the expectations that these surrounding institutions (community, kin, property) had of a couple served to keep the partners together throughout life, perhaps (in fact almost certainly) not happy, yet

> integrated within a firm social order. But then the couple terminated its association with these outside groups and strolled off into the dusk holding hands.'

Sentiment is much less likely than property to keep a marriage together over a lifetime.

In traditional societies, marriage was rooted in the community and in the wider family. In the patriarchal period of the Old Testament, for example, marriage was the cementing of a covenant between two wider kinship groups, and this integrated the couple into the community and its web of ties and expectations. In modern society, by contrast, marriage is rooted in sex and sentiment, a spontaneous feeling of personal affection, and this isolates the couple from former ties in the community and makes the couple a law unto itself. (The nearest thing we have to the traditional rooting of marriage in kinship and property is the case of royalty, in which marriages cement unions between royal houses, and this surrounds a royal marriage with ties and expectations that give it a quite exceptional stability. It is therefore unrealistic to elevate the royal family as a model and symbol of family life as is often done in Britain.)

This isolation of the modern nuclear family is enhanced by the consumer society. The individual family no longer needs contact with neighbours and the local community at the bus-stop, in the launderette, or at the pub, working men's club or cinema, because it owns its own car, washing machine, tumble dryer and colour telly. It need not even call in the plumber or the carpenter because of the availability of do-it-yourself equipment. This unprecedented opportunity for families to personally own virtually all the necessities for civilised living further isolates them from community ties. Not only does the sacred family fuel the fires of the consumer society, but also the consumer society props up the nuclear family. 'Do-it-yourself' is the hallmark not only of the enthusiastic handyman but of the typical modern family. 'We keep ourselves to ourselves' is the golden rule followed in each case.

Sadly and ironically, this moral and material isolation of the family is not just the hope of every young couple, it is also the downfall of many. With time, many couples find they just cannot stand it. Divorce is common not because the family is in decline but because our particular ideal of family life is all too popular. Calls for the upholding of family life are likely to be taken to mean the upholding of our society's isolated nuclear family, but this is the very thing that is a prime cause of marital breakdown.

Some Implications of Private Family Life

Some of the consequences of the modern isolated family have already been discussed: it keeps materialism and the consumer society thriving (ch. 2), it renders bereavement a particularly modern tragedy, and it is a prime cause of its own disintegration through divorce and separation. But there are many other aspects of modern society to which the privatised family contributes, and some of these aspects are none too healthy. Let us explore a few.

Theological implications

Theologically speaking, the creation of a home world and of a self-sufficient universe of meaning within the modern family is perhaps the prime way in which people in modern society protect themselves from the aloneness and lack of meaning that ensues from mankind's rejection of God (ch. 11). Curiously, the church colludes in this by marrying and baptising non-believers, thereby giving religious blessing to a form of family whose function is to protect its members from the Christian message[6].

The elevation of family life affects people's idea of what God is like. The idea of God as father is picked out from the multitude of biblical pictures of God, and this means not the patriarchal father of a whole nation of believers but the cosy, rather indulgent father of the private family, whose authority extends no further out into the world. People find it difficult to see what such a God might have to say to society as a whole, for they have fashioned an image of God as 'the private, independent being par excellence'[7]. He is the one who is there but who need not bother us much, and it is not surprising that in a scientific age many have come to see him as an unnecessary hypothesis.

A further theological implication concerns the church. Our society believes that the family has a monopoly on the exercise of love and that it is supremely in the family that love is to be shown and received. In so far as Christians accept this, and many do, it means that there is little love left over for the church; and so efforts to renew the church into truly caring communities experience difficulty. Members are too committed to their family to be committed to their church. The same commitment to one's own family also hits philanthropic endeavours – we cannot afford more than 10p for Oxfam because of the price of the Sunday family joint or of our children's shoes; we don't let out the spare room to help solve the housing shortage because we 'need' it for those few days a year when our grown-up children come to visit.

Political implications

We not only opt out of philanthropy but also citizenship. If the sense of powerlessness in the political arena is one of the things that makes the private world of the family so attractive, it is also true that our commitment to the family induces apathy towards politics. There has been much criticism of late of Christians not being sufficiently socially and politically involved, but probably they are no worse than anyone else; their lack of interest in politics may not be because they have a cosy home in heaven but because they have a cosy home on this earth in their suburban semi.

One important aspect of this opting out of civic responsibilities is the effect on cities, especially the dereliction of inner urban areas whose maintenance is of no interest to suburban owner-occupiers. As Lewis Mumford has put it: 'The city is nobody's business.'[8] This will be explored in the next chapter.

Law and Order

It is not only society at large that we do not feel responsible for; we do not even feel responsible for the families next door and certainly not for those a few doors away. This has had a profound effect on crime, especially juvenile crime. Perhaps the most effective deterrent in traditional societies is the informal network of community controls, such as gossip, that ensures that malefactors are detected and disciplined. An African friend described to me the way in which in his village, although in general parents discipline their own children, it is also quite legitimate for parents to discipline others' children; indeed, for this to happen is a great shame to the child's own parents and is one of the most effective sanctions. Contrast this with our society in which no adult would dare to lift a hand against someone else's child or act as community policeman. The street has become part of the public sphere, and therefore an area for which the individual is not responsible. It is for this reason that industrial societies have come to need police forces.

Many people believe that it is the lack of control by parents over their children that is the prime cause of the escalation of juvenile crime. Yet, looked at in the historical perspective of the transition from traditional communities to contemporary mass society, it is not the lack of control by parents over their *own* but over *others'* children that has opened up the possibility of large scale juvenile crime. One cannot possibly expect even the best parent to keep continual watch over his or her children; nor indeed can one expect every minute of a child's activities to be under the eagle eye of the local policeman or patrol car. Supervision of the minute-by-minute activities of children in the street and other public areas can only be through a sense of involvement on the part of every citizen. But with the channelling of the sense of responsibility into one's own nuclear family that is characteristic today, there is little chance of this happening. In any case the police would not want this to happen, for they strongly disapprove of individuals and communities 'taking the law into their own hands'. Although the police encourage the public to be more vigilant in the reporting of crime, the public are not supposed to take matters any further than reporting it to the police. Indeed, those modern communities which have taken law and order into their own hands (as in some parts of Ulster) are said to be in a state of anarchy in which law and order have broken down.

Personal Implications

The sense of having a place in the universe revolves around the world we construct within our own little families. This may be fine for those living in families (although as already indicated, often it is not so fine), but it leaves out in the cold those who are not in families – orphans, single people, widows, and old people. These are denied a socially approved place in our society. Every society has people who do not fit in, and they are generally those who fall outside the central social institution to which that society pays homage. But in our society this class is abnormally large, and this is because the central institution – the private family – is exclusive rather than inclusive. It is perhaps only when an individual finds himself in one of these outsider positions that he begins to see how important the family is in our society. The orphan, spinster or widow is left in no doubt that things are not as they should be and that they are deprived because they have no family. As with unemployment, it is when people are made to feel utterly bereft and cast aside that we know that we are on the track of an idol, in this case the family.

Since the sacred family is not necessarily a good thing, however, the position of being without a family, or at least of not living within a family, can for some people provide a chance to re-establish their social life on another, and perhaps more healthy, footing. This is certainly the experience of the young person leaving home, who may well experience a considerable degree of personal liberation and self-understanding. There is also some evidence to show that single old people who have never married are better off socially than those who were for most of their lives married. The never-married old person is unlikely to have put all his or her eggs socially into one basket and may have developed over the years a wide range of friends and interests which are relatively impervious to old age and to the death of any one of those friends.

The Role of Women

The cutting-off of the family from the community has largely reduced the roles of the married woman to those of wife and mother. The role of housewife is not necessarily a full-time occupation, and Mumford argues that the development of household furniture beyond the most rudimentary items took place only as the woman ceased to be involved in the husband's work; the care of furniture provided a new form of housework for the women of the well-off household. Even today, the interiors of peasant and crofting cottages are very simple, and this is not so much due to poverty, as to the women having better things to do all day than dust the furniture. Take this trend toward inventing housework into the present century and we find the modern housewife, chained to the kitchen sink and buying more and more 'time-saving' gadgets, which, far from saving time, generally add to the list of items to be cared for and serviced.

The care of children has also developed into something of supreme importance. A crucial factor here is the great decline in the infant mortality rate to virtually nil, which means that parents expect a newborn child to live to maturity and they are therefore able to invest considerable emotional resources in the nurture of the child. It is infinitely valuable in their eyes, and they spend their time coddling it and showing it off. A century or two ago, however, when the chances were more than even that a child would die before it was five years old, parents took the birth (and the death) of a child in a much more matter of fact way. Also, fewer children are needed today to replace the present generation, and so family sizes are much smaller, which means that parents, especially mothers, invest far more in far fewer children. A crucial member of the sacred family is the sacred child.

However, due to the problems inherent in this isolated family existence, many women long for a world outside the private world of family life. Hence the move out to work, for the reasons advanced in ch. 2. The important thing to note here is that, like their menfolk, they move into work not out of strength, as a free response, but out of the need to achieve something. In the case of women, that something may be friendship and sociability, confirmation of their sense of liberation, or extra money to furnish the family nest. Because they too enter work out of necessity rather than freedom, they are dependent on work and are exploitable (ch. 10).

Criticism of the Family

Since the private world of family life is coming to be recognised for the precarious thing that it is, not always able to provide confirmation for the individual's self, there has been a certain amount of debate about the family in recent years. One camp says that the family should be strengthened, although, as suggested above, if that means strengthening the conventional form of private family then this will only make things worse.

Another response accepts the conventional idea that the purpose of the family is to protect the identity of the individual, and goes on to argue that if the family is failing to do this then it must be replaced by, or at any rate supplemented by, other means toward the realisation of personal identity. This is a major theme in the work of the popular anti-psychiatrist R. D. Laing, whose case studies have shown the ways in which family life can stifle the individual so effectively that he has little option but to go mad as a way of escaping the pressures on him. This individualism is also a major theme in one wing of feminism in which individual personal development is seen as the prime human virtue, and conventional family life is acceptable only in so far as it promotes this. In the views of both Laing and the individualistic feminists, it may be in the interests of the development of the individual to leave his or her family, either temporarily or permanently.

Now although this is seen as abhorrent by many people who want to uphold family life, the essential similarity of both the conventional and the anti-conventional positions is remarkable. Both believe the family is or should be the place where the individual may be himself; the difference lies in their prescriptions of what to do when the individual finds that home is the one place where he can*not* be himself or herself. The traditional moralists say that the means (the family) should take precedence over the end (the individual), whereas the critics of the family claim it should be subordinated to the end of individual identity.

A far more radical, but less common, response is to criticise individual identity as the ultimate goal. The more collectivist and socialist wing of feminism tends toward this critique, and suggests that full personhood is not to be found in asserting one's individuality over and against others, but in a sense of solidarity with humanity as a whole, expressed in sisterhood (solidarity with all women) or in the revolutionary struggle (solidarity with the international working class as the representative of true humanity). This collectivist ideal sometimes finds expression in communal living, but it cannot be stressed enough here that most communes are essentially individualistic in that people join them in order to liberate themselves, to find themselves, and to be themselves as individuals, in not such a dissimilar way from that in which people get married.

Curiously, there is a streak of collectivism among those who defend the family. If the family is manifestly failing to meet the needs of the individual, people still argue that it is essential for the health of society. Thus the ultimate in terms of which one judges a social institution shifts from the individual to society as a whole. Many traditional moralists, among them the Festival of Light, argue that the family is 'the basic unit of society' and essential to 'the moral fibre of the nation'. With the family in decline, they say, society itself is in danger, and the precedent of the decline in moral standards prior to the fall of Rome is cited. A stable society is the ultimate goal.

Alongside Mary Whitehouse and the Archbishop of Canterbury lies a rather curious bedfellow, namely a certain brand of sociology. Embodied in Fletcher's book *The Family and Marriage in Modern Britain*, is the sociological school of thought called functionalism which was popular during the 1950s and early 1960s. In functionalism, society is compared to a biological organism, consisting of parts each of which fulfils a function for the organism (society) as a whole. Because a social institution exists it must have a function, and the ever-popular family was deemed no exception. Thus the family performs important functions for society, and it was argued that these should be recognised.

To sum up, the lines of debate have been drawn up in at least two ways. Firstly there are those who believe in the individual versus those who believe in society (either as it is now or as it will be after the revolution) as the yardstick by which to assess the family. This conflict will be looked at in more detail in ch. 5. Secondly, there is the divide between those who wish to preserve the status quo, who are unwilling to lose what we already have for the sake of a rather uncertain ideal future; and those who are committed to realising what they see as the potential of mankind, who see mankind in a process of 'becoming' such that we may never rest content with the present. These dimensions of individual vs. collective orientation, present vs. future orientation, clarify the plethora of polemics for and against the family: they unearth some of the commitments that underlie the polemics. Not that any one supporter or critic of the family should be forced into any one category; he may well display a combination of orientations, as is often the case with sociological ideal types.

The following quotation from Edmund Leach, for example, appears to criticise the family for its deleterious effects on both individual and society:

> 'The family looks in on itself; there is an intensification of emotional stress between husband and wife, and parents and children. . . . Far from being the basis of the good society, the family . . . is the source of all our discontents.'

Many people have seen the debate not in terms of collectivists vs. individualists or of present vs. future orientations, but in simple terms of those who are 'for' the family and those who are 'against' it. This is rather misleading; indeed, it is hard to know what is meant, for there has never been a society that did not include families. There is, however, a wide range of types of family from one society to another, and even within modern society, with its diverse social classes and ethnic groups, there are other family types than the isolated nuclear family (although this is the dominant one). The universal existence of families, together with wide variations in family type, means that it is pointless to suggest that the family might cease to exist. Some supporters of the family do talk in these terms, meaning, no doubt, that they fear the currently dominant family type may cease to exist. (The isolated nuclear family is in fact strongly supported by the economy and by the pattern of housing – it is so embedded in financial interests and in bricks and mortar that it is most unlikely to be on the point of collapse.)

Also, there is no such thing as '*the* family' in the abstract; men and women *will* continue to bear and rear children. The family only exists in so far as it is manifested in social relations between people. Yet an abstract notion of the family is often implied by those who attempt to elicit 'biblical teaching on the family' as though when the Bible mentions families it is referring to the same thing as when *we* talk about the family. This is to misunderstand both the nature of the family (a concrete and culturally variable thing) and the nature of the Bible (which talks in terms of concrete particulars rather than abstract principles). The Bible says much about the various forms of ancient Israelite family, and we can get glimpses of how faith was applied in those families and how the will of God expressed itself in them, and this can open our eyes to how faith may today be exercised in all kinds of situations[9]. But biblical teaching on an abstract, universal family there is not, because neither the family nor the Bible works that way. The question for today is not whether we are for or against the family but, first, what *kind* of family we want and, second, how *important* the family should be in relation to other social institutions.

Most people who are actually caught up in unhappy families do not in any case see things in abstract terms.

They make pragmatic responses to the opportunities and constraints of their situation, and it is for this reason that religious or political theorising and moralising of any kind are of relatively little use to those confronted with the urgent question of how to cope with an unhappy family life. Most people find some kind of escape possible; (the reason Laing's schizophrenics go mad is that they are among the few for whom there is no escape). The husband for whom family life has become flat may bury himself in his work, put in extra overtime, escape to the pub, or find a lady on the side. The housewife may escape from the sink by getting a job. The teenager may spend most of his free time outside the home, on the streets or in a youth club, in the belief that only there can he really be himself. Perhaps most poignant is the young person who tries to escape the tyranny of family life by leaving home and getting married himself. Much of the activity in which people are engaged is an escape from family life, an escape from an idol which has, in the manner of idols, demanded more than we are capable of giving.

The Family and Immortality

We have looked at the way in which, through the family, we create a sense of security and a sense of home, but the family is also one of the central ways in which people try to solve the problem of death. To understand the relation between the family and immortality we must look at kinship systems[10]. Relatives are defined differently in different cultures, and in all cultures (including our own) relatedness need not be genetic.

Whereas in our society we count forebears on both the father's and mother's side, there are many societies in which only one set of forebears counts. These are called 'unilineal' systems, since the lineage is passed on through only one sex. Thus in patrilineal societies people count only male forebears on their father's side (married women reckon their ancestors through the husband and his father). In matrilineal societies, it is through the female forebears of the mother (and for married men, through the mother-in-law). In patrilineal societies, the woman leaves her family and joins the lineage of the husband; in matrilineal societies, the man leaves his family and joins the lineage of his wife. (These again are 'ideal types' and no society is quite that simple.) It is therefore easy to recall one's ancestors for many generations since, instead of multiplying exponentially as in our system (I have 2 parents, 4 grandparents, 8 great-grandparents), there is only one ancestor per generation – in a patrilineal society it would be my father, his father, his father's father, and so on. This means that ancestors may live on in communal memory and folklore long after their physical death, and indeed, in many tribal societies ancestors play a crucial part in religion and in everyday life. Departed spirits can cause trouble in the here and now, and the minutiae of life may be subject to the approval of ancestors. Whereas in our society, keeping in touch with departed spirits is esoteric, mystical and potentially frightening because it delves into the unknown, in many tribal societies it is a very normal everyday occurrence; it may be no more frightening to know that one is ill because of the disapproval of the ancestors than it is for modern man to know that he is ill because of a germ. Both ancestors and germs have their own ritualised ways of being placated. In societies in which the presence of ancestors is all-pervasive, people can become truly immortal; death does not have the sting it so often does in modern society, because death does not cut one off from society.

In our kinship system in which we reckon descent through both our parents, we cannot keep track of all our relatives. Our ancestors multiply exponentially as we trace them back, so that an individual's ancestors and relatives number more than the population of his country! Clearly, some arbitary cut-off point must be adopted beyond which people are discounted as relatives. Our kinship system is thus extraordinarily messy by the standards of many unilineal systems in which to be a member of one lineage clearly distinguishes you from all other lineages. In our system, there is also a definite limit on the extent to which a person may be remembered in future generations, for unless we have done something extraordinary or been famous, we cannot expect our descendants to specially remember us along with all their other forebears. For modern man physical death is the start of social death. Our kinship system therefore puts a brake both on the extent to which we can place ourselves within society and on the extent to which we can perpetuate ourselves through our descendants.

This kinship system existed way back beyond the middle ages (no-one knows quite how it developed), and in those days it could even provide some sense of immortality. The handing down of farms, land, tools and skills from father to son gave a sense of continuity from one generation to the next. A father knew that his son would follow in his footsteps, and the son was only too glad to occupy the place held by his father. Indeed sometimes he would be only too eager to get his father out of the way so that he could take over the family farm or workshop. With the rise of individualism, however, offspring now want to strike out and find an identity that is all their own rather than handed down from parents, and in general parents concur in this. This means that sooner or later the parents lose moral authority over the offspring, whereas in traditional society the old often had authority until their dying day. As Shorter puts it[11]:

> 'Adolescents now soon realise that they are not links in a familial chain stretching across the ages. Who they are and what they become is independent (at least so they believe) of who their parents are. And they themselves are responsible for what their children become only to the point of seeing that they march into the future with straight teeth. The chain of generations serves no larger moral purpose for adolescents, and therewith the moral authority of parents over their growing children collapses.'

Those who bemoan the decline in parental authority or the loss in status of the old are often those very same people who exalt the individual; they would do well to ponder that this very exaltation of the individual is to some extent the cause of the decline in parental and elderly authority.

Nevertheless, there is still much that parents hand down to their children. At the least, a name is handed down, usually along with earthly possessions. This is seen by people as only right and natural. We also feel that we have to pass on to children both earned and inherited wealth. Although we may agree in theory that the rich should not be able to keep vast wealth within one family for generations, we always claim *we* are not among the rich (only 'comfortably off') and we complain when the taxman stops us handing everything on to *our* children. What is the point of working, we demand, if we cannot hand on the fruits of our labours? It is not only the present but also the future family that gives meaning to work.

But it is not just a name and wealth that we hand on. Statistical studies have shown the likelihood of children inheriting other things from their parents: – social class, income level, level of education, values, prejudices, expectations of a spouse, child-rearing methods, and so on. Although much of this is unintentional, and parents are often distressed to see their faults as well as their good points re-emerging in their children, a good deal of this handing on of parental life-style is conscious. Parents may feel it essential that their children go to the right school and get a good job; or, if they are at the bottom of the social scale, that they go to the local school and do not get 'stuck up'.

Often parents try to make up in the next generation for what they themselves lacked. The modern individual, distancing himself from his everyday roles because they are at best uninspiring and at worst dehumanising, may centre his notion of his real self on what he would like to have done had he had the opportunity, rather than on what he has actually done. He or she then puts pressure on the children to achieve these dreams, and if they conform and achieve the dream, then the parent's self-identity, which was a fantasy of his own life, becomes reality in the life of the offspring. In this way, the real self is granted a kind of immortality, and physical death can perhaps be faced with greater equanimity. Nevertheless, this kind of vicarious living through one's children is not really approved of, and psychiatrists' couches are littered with the children of such parents. But its frequency suggests that the need for a lasting identity and the need to leave behind something of oneself are widespread.

In any society each generation passes its culture on to the next. The social mechanisms by which this is done vary from one society to another – in many traditional societies, it is the family together with the local community, while in modern western societies it is largely the family together with the school. The family is crucial in reproducing not only the species but also culture; even though the individual dies, he knows that his body will be outlived by his culture and his values, albeit with minor modifications. He may not be able to perpetuate life, but he can perpetuate what he has lived for. In periods of rapid social change, however, this may not be possible, and it can be distressing for older people to realise that their values and culture, as well as their body, may not be immortal.

This chapter has looked at the family as an institution that provides a sense of being at home in the world and a measure of immortality. The precise way and the effectiveness with which the family does this varies from one society to another. In our own society, people look to the family more for a sense of home than of immortality; viewed in historical perspective, today's family is perhaps not so effective in providing either a home or a place in eternity. Design faults in the modern mass-produced family do not, however, render it any the less popular.

4
The Suburban Dream

The previous chapter suggested that the small private family is the dominant family type in modern society; this chapter will look at suburbia as the dominant pattern of living within cities and towns. Just as actors need the right scenery if their play is to be convincing, so the drama of family life is enhanced by the right setting. Marital bliss, mid-twentieth century style, is hardly possible if one is sharing a house with in-laws and a motley array of distant relatives, if one's dwelling is under the same roof as a noisy factory (as with the traditional craftsman), or if one lives in a remote part of the country with few mod. cons. and is forced into co-operation with neighbours (as with the traditional peasant). The ideal house today is detached, with its own garden and all mod. cons., and the ideal location is (or was) suburbia. Let's take suburbia first.

Sub-urbia is a place mid-way between the city and the country, and ideally embodies the best of both worlds. The attitude of the modern private family toward the city is mixed. On the one hand the city is the source of employment and livelihood; it is a lively place, where there is entertainment, high culture, the best shops. It is a free place where one is not constrained by tradition, where the young person may be himself, where the individual may voluntarily lose himself in the anonymity of the crowd. But the city also has its disadvantages. Its very diversity and cosmopolitan nature mean that it contains all kinds of alien elements which threaten the private world of the family – adults may feel they can keep at bay the undesirable elements of other social classes, other ethnic groups, down-and-outs, and petty criminals but, they wonder, can the children be protected too? Will undesirable children go to the same school? Will one's own children be molested on the way home from school? The city is an exciting place, but it is no place to bring up children; so feels the private family.

What about feelings for the country as a place to live? This has manifest advantages for raising a family; it is cleaner, healthier, and safer, and the children need not be under constant supervision. It provides an orderly and predictable world which, it may be hoped, can mesh with the private world of the family. But it is in this very orderliness that the other side of the coin emerges – village life entails precisely those ties from which the modern individual and his family are trying to escape. Village tradition is the opposite of the freedom of the city; the village seems 'dead' to the modern individual.

The upper middle class of the nineteenth century caught on to an idea that various wealthy classes had held on and off for two thousand years. This was the idea of combining the best of city and country in a home on the outskirts of the city, close to or in the country. Aided by the railway companies, by speculative builders, and in the 1920s and 30s by mortgages from rapidly expanding building societies, this ideal gained enormous popularity; thus came into being the now most obvious feature of the modern city, at least as seen from the air: sprawling suburbia.

Along with this change in the desired location, there came a change in the kind of house people wanted to live in. The middle-class Victorian house had been a large rented villa, with ample space for aged grandparents, odd relations and servants. This became more and more unsuitable as the modern private family emerged, and for two reasons. Firstly, it did not provide enough privacy from in-laws and lodgers. My father, for example, remembers the joy with which at the turn of the century his mother viewed their removal out of such a house into a smaller and more self-contained dwelling; for the first time she could be in charge of her own home.

This leads us to the second, and related, aspect of the Victorian house. The family did not have control over the stage on which was enacted the supposedly private drama of family life, not only because of the presence of mother-in-law but also because of the hovering presence of the landlord in the background. At the turn of the century, about 90% of households in Britain lived in privately rented accommodation; by the early 1970s this had fallen to around 10%. Slightly over half the households today are owner-occupied with virtually total control over what they do in and with their houses, and rather under half are in publicly rented council houses where they are both more secure and more free than the private tenant.

Exit the large rented Victorian house complete with basement and attic in which to store servants, maids and mother-in-law; enter the two-storey, three-bedroomed detached house with modern kitchen and manageable garden. This, at any rate, became the ideal in the building society promotion literature. Many had to be satisfied with less than the ideal, and the characteristic products of the building boom of the 1920s and 30s were the mortgaged semi and the semi-detached council house. The twin ideals of privacy for the family and control over the home by the family were embodied not only in new forms of tenure, but also in the physical structure and contents of the house. The garden and the fence surrounded the house with a protecting membrane a good deal more effective than the dividing wall of the nineteenth century terraced house. The detached house came to be preferred to the semi for it could be surrounded totally by garden. The garden itself provided a semblance of the countryside, while the house (with mains drainage, telephone, electricity and gas) had all the advantages of civilisation. The house was crammed fuller and fuller with gadgetry and comforts (washing machine, telly, fitted carpets, deep freeze, central heating and so on) so that the family came to be less and less dependent on the outside world, although it has come to be more and more dependent on outsiders to service this range of machinery and comforts.

Around the ideals of privacy and control, a 'housing ladder' developed: the family in privately rented accommodation have their name down for a council house, the council house family may be saving up for a mortgage or may buy their house from the council, the family in a mortgaged terrace house aspire to a semi in a better area, and the family in a semi aspire to a detached house in a better area still. Getting the ideal house in the ideal place is a difficult matter, for not everyone can be in the ideal place at the same time, and so most people find themselves a bit too far out of town or a bit too far in, in a house that's a bit too old and decayed or a bit too new and small. Reverse ladders have also developed as people move back into the city centre in order to do up old terraced houses in their search for roots, style, and individuality.

The less control one has over the house as a whole, for example the council tenant compared to the mortgage holder, the more likely one is to fill the house with gadgetry and comforts which create an environment able to sustain one's image of a world under one's private control. The middle class person, apt to criticise the working class for their accumulation of 'unnecessary' goods on hire purchase, may do well to ponder whether he might not do the same were he to lose his mortgaged house. What the mortgage does for the middle class, hire purchase does for the working class – enabling the family to create an environment all their very own, which they can call 'home', and which reinforces the solidity of the world they want to believe in[1].

This ideal of a private environment over which one has total control, and the extent to which it has become embodied in bricks and mortar, became clear the other day when I was sitting in the kitchen gazing out of the window. Inside the window was an environment ordered to suit my own needs – cooker, fridge, shelves all where I wanted them, the food I liked in the larder, my favourite tablecloth on the table, curtains I had chosen on the window, paint I had chosen on the walls. Outside the window was a view of houses and fields and roads over which I had no control whatsoever. For me, living in a mortgaged flat with no garden, the cut-off point was the window; with a garden, the cut-off point would have been the garden hedge. Try this for yourself – look out of the window and see where the boundary is; if you are a student in a hall of residence or digs, the cut-off point will be even nearer to you – you may be free to arrange the furniture and put things on the wall, but you are not free to paint the wall itself, so the boundary for you is the surface of the wall itself. If you are in hospital, even your own body is not private and under your control, but you do maintain a place over which you do have control and that is your locker. Most readers should be able to identify a sharp cut-off point between the area over which they and their family have control and the area beyond, which is not under their control. This is the physical embodiment of the division between the private and the public which formed so central a part of the discussion of family life and individualism in the previous chapter.

This sharp cut-off point is not universal throughout the world. In a tribal or nomadic group, the person identifies with the community and feels he shares with the community a joint control over their territory. Even beyond the village the environment is not necessarily alien, for the villagers may see the surrounding forest as their traditional hunting ground or the savanna as their traditional grazing land.

The growth of the modern city in which the individual and his family feel they have inalienable control over a tiny area and virtually none over a much larger area is at the root of many of our urban problems, and some of these will now be examined.

Effects of Suburbia on the Rest of the City

Many suburban dwellers are very happy with suburbia; they may not have achieved their ideal, but they are content with their particular compromise between country and city, and they have found ways of making up for any lack of privacy and control. But the creation of the suburbanite's environment entails costs that other parts of the city have to bear:

1. *The ghetto and the slum*

The process by which people move out of town in search of the suburban ideal has been aptly named *leapfrogging*. The Victorian middle classes who first moved out of town to the suburbs found that beyond the over-large villas from which they desired to move had grown up perhaps a mile or more of artisan housing and industry, and they had to leapfrog over this in order to arrive at the boundary between city and country. It was for this reason that suburbia could never develop on any scale until the railway had been invented. Then in the inter-war period, the lower-middle class over which the previous generation had jumped found that a mortgage was within their reach too, and so they had to jump over the original suburbanites in order to find the lots on which speculative builders were creating a new promised land. A similar jump had to be made if land was to be found for municipal housing (one result of which was that by the early 1950s commuting costs along with higher rents made many dwellers in these new estates financially worse off than those still living in older housing nearer the city). Many of the original upper-middle class suburban families now found themselves surrounded by a sea of mediocre housing and lower social classes, and so set off again in search of the rural idyll, this time to newly commuterised villages even further out. By this time, the deadening hand of village tradition was itself dead, and so now village life embodies the ideal blend of security and freedom.

Now an important aspect of this leapfrogging is that people leave behind them housing which no longer meets their needs. Left behind are whole areas of housing which were built for the needs of earlier generations and which may not really meet anyone's needs today. Classic examples are to be found in the areas of large Victorian houses left behind by the original suburbanites. Designed for large families with servants, these houses have been taken over by groups at the bottom of the housing ladder who cannot afford purpose-built housing. The low prices and low rents of such unwanted housing make it the only option for those who do not have savings for a mortgage or who do not qualify for a council house. Immigrants often do not qualify for either – they may send anything left over from earnings home to support relatives, and local councils may demand a number of years' residence in the city before applicants can be allocated a council house. Also, the fact that almost all new housing is built for small family occupation means that those who do not live in families or who live in larger extended families have little option but to move to these old evacuated areas. The needs of many immigrants who still want to live an extended family life, and of single people such as students who want a small flat or bedsitter are met by the adaptation of these large old houses. The support given by society to the small isolated family is perhaps nowhere better illustrated than in the design of new housing for this kind of family, leaving all the worst and oldest housing to those who want to live alone, with non-family members, or in an extended family.

The physical state of these older areas can quickly deteriorate. Often privately rented, neither tenant nor landlord have much interest in maintaining the decaying fabric; the occupants are unlikely to be well represented on the local council and so public facilities are likely to deteriorate; and a mixed population of students, immigrants and a few remaining elderly widows is unlikely to have many interests in common and to work together to keep the area viable.

Perhaps most important, residents see the place only as a temporary residence, as a zone of transition[2]. The immigrant family may have moved there as the only available place on entry to the country, but does not see it as permanent. The single person supposes he will someday get married and move out. The student supposes he will qualify and move on to better things. The elderly widow looks back at better things and forward to the grave, so she too is in a period of transition. There is therefore little commitment to the area and no incentive for residents to invest time, energy or money in it.

And so these areas run down, which helps to give immigrants, students and landlords a bad name, for they are each supposed to be responsible for the squalor and decay. The idolising by councils, building societies and speculative builders of the small private family as the only living arrangement worth financing and building decent new housing for, is, in fact, more responsible.

Thus the slum and ghetto are created. Exit the large

Victorian house; enter not just suburbia, but suburbia plus the slum.

2. *The abandoning of the city centre*

Many of the problems of the ghetto pertain also to the city centre. A resident population of immigrants, students and young people could provide a vibrant and innovative core for city life, yet these people all see themselves as merely passing through, on the way to higher things, and so the city centre is pervaded by a sense of dereliction and impermanence rather than excitement and innovation.

But city centres have other problems. Here were once the rows of artisan cottages of the early industrial revolution, now demolished and replaced by inner ring roads and flats. I will not dwell here on the issue of high-rise living, for this is a chapter about suburbia, and suburbia has led not to high-rise, but to the need for vast areas of the inner city to be reduced to motorways and car parks. Suburbia developed around the railway, indeed almost all our urban land was developed around the railway; but the motor car, like the mortgage and the council house, offered the individual and his family something the railway could not – privacy and control. So the steam-hauled commuter of the nineteenth century became the motorised commuter of the twentieth; and in the process vast areas of housing had to be demolished to make way for the private environment on four wheels of the private individual on his way to work for his private family. The nearer he gets to the city centre, the more congested it becomes, and the more asphalt-covered land is needed for parking. The city has literally bowed down to the idol of the private individual.

In addition to the ghetto and motor-induced demolition, a third inner-city problem that derives partly from the suburban dream is that the city centre is where a large number of people work. Now this would not be a problem, were it not for the phenomenon described in chapter 2, that people work for their families. The meaning of work is found outside work. This means that people are less concerned about their work environment than their home environment, and so no one is concerned to speak up for the inner city. It also means that high-class housing, belonging to those who are able to choose, is far removed from the place of work. So alongside the prestige office blocks designed to impress the firm's clients – environments as advanced in some ways as any known to technological man – there are areas of decay and dereliction about which no-one seems concerned.

What is draining life out of the city centre and out of 'zones of transition' is the ideal of the private family and its enshrinement in housing policy, not least the policies of the building societies. So long as society believes in the private family, and there is little sign of any large-scale move away from this, and so long as we continue to build houses and roads almost entirely for that form of family, then city centres are going to face intractable problems. No amount of pouring of resources and money into the city centre can do more than a first-aid, patch-up job. Unfortunately, this does not seem to be realised by many planners and politicians who continue to talk and act as though the problems of the inner city can be solved merely with reference to the inner city.

It is also becoming fashionable for Christians to move into such areas, responding to Jesus' command to be alongside the poor and needy. But, in the climate in which planners and politicians talk about the problems of the inner city, it is likely that Christians will simply tack the theological concepts of incarnation and witness in the inner city on to the contemporary fantasy that by investing enough money and personnel in the inner city it will become a good place to live in. If they want to solve the problems of the inner city then they have to demonstrate alternative ideals to those which exalt the individual and private family life. But even were society's ideals to change radically and rapidly (which is unlikely), the old ideals would still be embodied in the housing stock and it would be a century or more till we could erase the legacy of the private family. This is not to say that Christians and others should not be with the poor and oppressed in the inner city; they should. But if they think this injection of manpower will in itself solve the problems of the inner city, then they are simply conforming to the conventional wordly wisdom.

No-one can draw a blueprint for a perfect urban environment, for there are limits to the extent to which cities can be planned. But we can ensure that, even if there is one form of family life which dominates society at present, we should not build housing totally for that family type. We should build a range of houses of different sizes and in different sorts of locations; ideals do change over time, and it is an embarrassment to be lumbered with a housing stock totally geared to the requirements of a past ideal. Once built, houses are rather inflexible things, and so it is worthwhile building in flexibility and variety at the start. There is, thankfully, some indication that a more varied housing stock is being preserved, as a result of the present interest in rehabilitating rather than demolishing older housing. Future generations may thank us for this, not so much because they will necessarily share our fad for conservation and restoration but because we will have handed on to them at least a few variations from the three-bedroomed family house.

3. *Social apartheid*

In the middle ages, the urban craftsman shared his home with his apprentices; they ate together at the same table and perhaps all slept together in the same room, or even in the same bed. By the nineteenth century, maids and servants still lived in the same house as their masters, but ate separately in the basement and had separate quarters in basement or attic. If the nineteenth century middle class banished the working class to the basement, the twentieth century has banished them to the other side of town altogether. Modern cities are characterised by homogeneous housing zones; here a classy suburban area, there a council housing estate. When these zones attain the size of a school catchment area there are serious consequences for it means that children grow up entirely with children of their own social class; and even without zones of that size, the absence of children of other social classes from the house and the street means that out-of-school playmates are likely to be of the same social background. This creates a form of apartheid based on social class as effective as that based on race which is practised in South Africa; more effective perhaps because the child is not aware of it.

Thus, an important ideological change has taken place since the last century. Then, the middle classes frequently saw how the other half lived. They knew that the standard of living of their servants was inferior to their own, and in the streets it was not possible to avoid at least some awareness of poverty and squalor (although the actual measure of this poverty was not fully known until the publicity efforts of social surveyors and the Salvation Army in the last two decades of the century). The nineteenth century was acutely aware of social and economic *inequality*, and developed an ideology to justify this inequality: the ideology of laissez-faire capitalism which claimed that those with wealth had achieved it through their own hard work and talents, while poverty had descended simply through personal fecklessness. In the mid-twentieth century, however, the middle classes in general simply do not know how the other half lives, and have adopted an ideology which says that there is no inequality or that we are well on the way to eradicating inequality. The working class, by contrast, are constantly made aware of how the better-off live through advertising and television, and this helps sustain the working class 'us and them' view of society in which inequality is recognised.

To amplify the analogy with South Africa, their system of racial apartheid is nearer our nineteenth century than our twentieth century version. The white South African child may well have a black nanny and play with her black children, entailing contact not unlike that of the nineteenth century British child with nannies and social inferiors, and so as he grows up an ideology is needed which justifies his privileged position. By contrast, twentieth century British and American social apartheid is rather more effective since it hides from view the very existence of inequality.

This separation of the well-off from the less well-off has

important moral implications. Consider the parable of the Good Samaritan who took pity on the man fallen among thieves that other passers-by had ignored. Today, it is unlikely that the would-be Samaritan would even find himself on the same road as the needy, for all his personal and social needs are met within his own house and middle-class locality. He has no reason to venture near the poor and materially needy. It is significant that the organisation that has taken its name from this parable, the Samaritans, occupies an office, and has to be reached by telephone. Nowadays, the 'fallen among thieves' has to come to the Samaritans – a fundamental reversal of Jesus's parable. Anyone who is concerned today to love his neighbour should examine his own position in the urban structure to see whether he has set out on a road on which he is unlikely to meet his needy neighbour. Seen in this light, the movement of socially concerned suburbanites back into the inner city with its high level of people in need is admirable, although movement into solid working class areas may be fraught with difficulties and dishonesties on both sides.

Curiously, there is something to be said here in favour of the rather archaic geographical boundaries of the Anglican parish and the archaic locations of a good many churches of any denomination. In older urban areas in which there has been demolition, rebuilding, leapfrogging and reverse leapfrogging, the geographical boundaries of responsibility of many churches no longer fit any currently definable neighbourhood. Rather than being a problem, though, this provides a unique opportunity since the local church may end up as the only group of people in the area committed to serving all its neighbours, whoever they may be. It may seem messy for the parish to include a corner of a council estate in another borough, a select commuter zone, and odd bits and pieces of older mixed housing, but it provides an unprecedented opportunity for people to exercise love towards neighbours from whom they would otherwise be separated by social divisions.

The private family is to be criticised, not so that the community can be idolised in its place, but because it is isolationist. When this is expressed in homogeneous housing zones and by consumer goods such as cars and televisions which come to be regarded as necessities, people get cut off from their neighbours whether or not they themselves believe in the private family. Jesus said that 'love your neighbour as yourself' was second only to the command to 'love the Lord your God'. Several times Jesus mentioned that family commitments can come between a person and following Him, and had he lived today he might have mentioned also that the family as we know it now comes between us and our neighbour.

Is the Dream Becoming a Nightmare?

So much for some of the problems that suburbia is causing, or at least exacerbating, in other parts of the city. But what about suburbia itself? Despite the evident satisfaction of many of its inhabitants, there are strong indications that suburbia is causing problems for them too. The main one is that suburbia has become too popular. The suburban ideal of the ideal house in the ideal position is clearly something that only a select few can attain. When everyone strives for it, most people end up with something less than the ideal. Land prices escalate, and so houses and gardens become smaller: the house becomes a mere 'box', with the garden 'no more than a pocket handkerchief'. The ideal view of woods and fields is reduced to the view of the next row of boxes at the end of a tiny garden. But it is not just increasing prices and decreasing plot sizes that accompany popularity. A few of the other problems that suburban popularity breeds will be examined now.

1. *Transport*

The growth of suburbia beyond the wildest dreams of the early speculators has led to the transport problems that characterise modern western cities. Of course, the mid-Victorian city, and even ancient Rome, had traffic congestion and traffic-induced pollution and noise. But the wonders of technology and social planning in this century, far from eradicating this typically urban problem, have magnified it beyond belief. Many of the costs are born by those who live in or near the city centre, but congestion is not without costs for the commuters themselves. The journey to and from work may lengthen the effective working day to ten or eleven hours, so that the man arrives home with little energy and even less time for his family, for whose sake he is supposedly making this daily expedition.

Increasing fuel costs and train fares have more subtle consequences – they constantly shift the location of the ideal home; the ideal upper-middle class commuter residence of the 1960s is now altogether too expensive to commute to daily. This precariousness of the ideal home meshes with the precariousness of the ideal marriage described in the previous chapter; just as the family drama may be disrupted by internal strains, so the setting for the family drama may be threatened by external forces such as the increasing price of oil or the disintegration of the public transport system. The problem is not just that commuting costs *have* changed, it is also the ever-present possibility that they *may* change in future; an element of unpredictability is built in, such that the modern family can be no more sure that its house will remain worth living in than it can be sure that the family itself will remain worth living in. The nearer the suburban ideal one gets, the more precarious one's position becomes; the ideal is at the very outer limits of the city, yet these limits are largely affected by factors such as commuting costs and times. The ideal location is more prone to changes in these factors than are compromise locations nearer the city, so occupation of the ideal home is associated with uncertainty and a fear of being dislocated from one's pre-eminent position.

A consequence of the gobbling up of land by suburbia that perhaps affects more the compromise dweller of middle suburbia than the privileged member of outer suburbia is that, whereas once suburbia was to provide the ideal blend of city and country, now it provides neither. It takes so long to get to both city and country that, apart from necessities such as work, many families find it not worth the effort. Suburbia has become starved of amenities like local cinemas, and there is little left to replace the city centre opera house and theatres which have become too remote for regular patronage. But the country too is becoming more remote as building eats up more and more of the green belt. Setting out to achieve the best of both worlds, the suburbanite ends up with perhaps the worst of both worlds.

2. *Uniformity*

Whereas in its early days suburbia was advertised as providing a uniquely favoured environment which the private family could make its very own, now its popularity means that the word 'suburban' is the very epitome of sameness, uniformity and dullness. This poses serious threats to the ideal of the private family. The expectation of modern marriage is that two unique individuals spontaneously join their personalities to create a unique world of their own. It is rather difficult to sustain this illusion if one lives in a house identical to all the others in the street, which is in turn identical to all the others in the neighbourhood. Not that suburbia causes marital breakdown, but it certainly does provide an appropriate setting for the feeling that one's marriage has become a matter of conforming to the expectations of others and that the expression of one's individual identity is stifled.

Suburban dwellers do their utmost to express their individuality in their houses. Although a walk along the street shows houses of stunning uniformity, a stroll along the back footpath or a ride in the train going past the backs immediately shows a different picture. One house has an extension, another a home-made potting shed, another has the lawn dug up for vegetables, another is a veritable museum of plastic gnomes. Do-it-yourself has the appeal that for once you will be doing something that your next door neighbour will not; but the irony is that your piece of practical identity construction will likely be employing the very same model of Black and Decker and the very same sort of Christmas gift tool kit as the neighbour[3]. Suburbia typifies the problem of the individual in mass society – he wants to be different from everyone else, to derive his identity from his differences from other people, but the means that a mass-market consumer society offer him for expressing his differences are also marketed to millions of his neighbours.

3. *The fear of overcrowding*

The private world of suburbia is as precarious as the private world of the modern family. Just as the private family feels threatened by unknown outside forces, so the suburbanite fears that outsiders will take over the neighbourhood. And the historical evidence of urban leapfrog is that sooner or later as people move out of a neighbourhood it will indeed become inundated by outsiders and its character changed. The suburbanite accepts the people and houses present when he moved into the area, but he will fight to the last against any future addition of people and houses into the neighbourhood. This is the trouble with privacy – no sooner have you achieved it than you have to start defending it.

Fear that a neighbourhood will become 'spoiled' through 'overcrowding' may be expressed in hostile attitudes toward readily identifiable immigrants. But it may also be projected into a more general fear of overcrowding – of the nation and of the world as a whole. At a time when there is net emigration, when nutritional standards are higher than ever, and when city centres are less densely populated than they have been for decades, it is striking that people in countries like Britain should believe their country to be overcrowded and be worried about immigration. Much of this fear derives from the threatened privacy of the private family and of the suburban house; unable to safeguard that privacy, we project our fear of overcrowding onto the nation as a whole. Nor is it surprising that popular books on ecology claiming the whole world to be overcrowded find an eager readership in middle class suburbanites in whom the fear of overcrowding – the fear of more people – is deeply ingrained.

4. *The rush to the countryside*

As the suburban environment seems less and less able to provide the right setting for the private world of the family, so there has begun a frantic search for new environments, even if only the temporary environment of the holiday in the sun in Southern Europe. In addition to the appeal of elusive sunshine, there are also clear romantic overtones in the promotional literature for such holidays. Suburbia may be uniform, overpopulated and hardly the place for developing individuality, but on a Mediterranean beach holding hands in the sunset – here surely is a setting in which the unique love between two individuals can flourish.

The countryside, too, has been discovered. The growth of suburbia means that living near the country is no longer possible for many, but it is possible to visit the countryside at holidays and at weekends, and for those who can afford it, the second home in the countryside is the perfect complement to the pad in town. The trouble is that the very same things are sought in the countryside as in suburbia, namely privacy, freedom and getting away from everybody else. Once everybody starts striving for these things, the very same problems emerge in the countryside (especially on a public holiday) that have plagued suburbia for half a century. Beauty spots become overcrowded, long-standing visitors feel such spots are being 'spoiled' by new visitors, and there are traffic jams on the roads. And curiously, just as the planners of the inner city fail to go to the root of the problem in the ideals of suburban individualism and privacy, so the new breed of countryside planners seems to believe that the invasion of the countryside can be handled simply by better management of the countryside[4].

5. *No place for the old*

If today's housing stock is geared toward the needs of the small private family, what happens to the suburbanite when he has grown old, children left home, and spouse died? There is little desire on either side for him or more likely her to go to live with adult offspring; most likely she will continue living on her own in a house that is now far too big and difficult to manage. Sooner or later, and the size and unsuitability of the house often mean sooner, she finds coping on her own too much, and is cajoled away into an old folks' home. In the meantime, valuable family-sized accommodation has been unavailable for the use for which it was intended.

Conclusion

This chapter has looked at suburbia as an attempt to mould the physical environment to provide a home that staves off the homelessness that plagues the human condition. This typifies the way the natural environment is used by mankind, and it matches the way in which culture is used to solve the problem of homelessness.

5
Individualism Rules – Or Does It?

Earlier chapters described the modern private family and suburbia as life-support systems for the private individual; the sacred family is like an altar situated within a larger temple devoted to the worship of the individual. The work ethic and the church are other altars in this temple. In modern Western societies, people believe in the individual as an ultimate value.

There are a few noisy dissenters, though. Some critics of the family, of work and of the church believe that the individualism which is usually relied on to render these institutions meaningful cripples their real task and function. Critics believe modern society to be absurdly devoted to the happiness of the individual as the sole aim in life.

At the same time, many who believe in individualism criticise society for going to the opposite extreme. The Nobel Prize winner Milton Friedman is not the only economist to believe that the West is in danger of killing off freedom and democracy as a result of the way in which free enterprise is being controlled and taken over by the state; the economy is becoming more and more *collectivised*, they say, and this is threatening the freedom of the individual. Others claim that the welfare state takes away freedom of choice from the individual and undermines the individual's responsibility for his own welfare. This is the argument against the welfare state in America, while in Britain the abolition of private beds in National Health Service hospitals and governmental measures against private education have been criticised on the same grounds. Nor are the media immune from charges of creeping collectivism; many fear the BBC is becoming controlled by a clique of left-wing intellectuals who are slowly conditioning viewers into collectivism (curiously, other critics despair at the inherent conservatism of the BBC!)

Put in these terms it seems that the critics of individualism are left wing and the critics of collectivism are right wing. But the camps are not necessarily drawn up along these conventional political lines. The New Left object not only to rampant individualism but also to the centralised power of the state, whether it be communist or democratic. There is a certain fellow feeling between British and American politicians of the right who object to the collectivisation of the economy by the state, and Chinese communist leaders who are aiming to develop more local autonomy within China and object to the even more heavy-handed rule by the Soviet state. And in 1939 the capitalist West went to war to defend its freedom and its individualism not against Stalinist socialism but against right-wing fascism.

In general, what seems to be happening worldwide is a certain collectivising of society by states of every political hue, and whether objections come from those wearing a right- or a left-wing hat depends on the particular political history of the nation concerned. Since in Britain and America these champions of the individual have tended in recent decades to be of the right, we have come to believe that there is an inherent association between individualism and the right, and between collectivism and the left. But these stereotyped labels of 'left' and 'right' do not clarify the subject of this chapter – the phenomenon of individualism versus collectivism in modern industrial society.

It is curious that in Western (and also many eastern bloc) countries there are those who deeply believe society has succumbed to the evil of collectivism, while at the same time there are those who equally deeply and sincerely castigate society for the continuing espousal of its individualistic inheritance. Is one side right and the other wrong? No, they are both right and wrong. They are each right in identifying the existence within society of elements of individualism and elements of collectivism to an historically unprecedented degree. But they are wrong in averring that the solution to collectivism is to reassert the value of the individual, or that the solution to individualism is collectivisation. Expanding this rather perplexing statement is the purpose of this chapter.

Polarisation

It is true that there are strong tendencies toward *collectivism* in modern humanist industrial societies. One tendency derives from the nature of *technology* itself. The classic laissez-faire economic model of supply and demand supposed that, in a perfect economy, increased demand for a product would lead to increased supply. This supposed that the supplier could respond to the demand more or less immediately. In practice, of course, this is rarely possible – even in a simple agricultural economy it takes a year to increase grain production and two to three years to increase livestock production, by which time the demand may have changed again. As technology becomes more complex it takes longer and longer to respond to demand. To produce a new model of car takes between five and ten years from the initial decision to go ahead to the rolling off the production line of the first standard cars for sale. Development of an aircraft takes longer, and putting a man on the moon longer still. And if a country decides to go ahead with such projects but has no existing motor or aerospace industry on which to build, then the time lag may be measured in decades rather than years.

If it takes so long to respond to demand, then it is no use industry simply responding to demand; it has to create and manipulate demand, so that when the finished product is ready there will be a market willing to purchase it. To this end it is also essential that there be a stable economic climate. An economy oscillating unpredictably between boom and slump is disastrous in a highly technologised world, since decisions to expand will be made in times of boom with a high chance that slump conditions will prevail when the product is ready for selling. An industry that gets its fingers burned more than once is likely to become less and less willing to invest at all, even in boom times. It is also essential for industry that inflation be kept at a low and steady level, or else it will prove impossible to estimate future costs, and investment decisions will not be made rationally.

The need for economic stability is one reason for industrial mergers and the growth of the multi-national corporation. If a firm can buy up both its suppliers and those to whom it sells then it will be able to control and stabilise both supply and demand; by diversifying into a range of products, sold and produced in a range of countries, it hedges its bets and minimises the cost to the firm of a slump in any one country or in any one product. But even the diversified multi-national company knows that it cannot totally guarantee economic stability, and so the growth of the multi-national has been accompanied by increasing pressure on national governments to take responsibility for providing economic stability. Thus when an essential industry, such as coal, steel or the railways, goes to the wall as a result of market pressures, the government is expected to step in with either subsidies or nationalisation, for the collapse of such industries would be catastrophic for many other sectors of the economy. Governments are also charged with responsibility for maintaining exchange rates at a steady level, and for keeping down inflation and unemployment. Organisations such as the EEC attempt to provide stability on the international as well as the national level. The foreign policies of the major powers are geared largely toward maintaining political, and therefore economic, stability in those countries with which they trade.

To sum up, the complexity of modern technology necessitates rational planning, and rational planning necessitates a predictable and stable economic future. This can be achieved only through governmental control of the national and international economic order. Which means that the economy becomes more and more collectivised.

There is another factor behind the desire to plan. This is the belief that mankind (both collectively and individually) has the right and the responsibility to control its own future. Philosophically the driving force behind this belief is humanism, and politically the driving forces are the ideologies of (in the West) democracy and (in the East) socialism. If man is to control his own destiny, then this requires planning – planning not only of the economy but also of society. Democratically elected governments do not like too frequent elections, and communist governments do not like them at all, partly because the possibility of defeat in an election jeopardises the carrying out of the will of the people that the current government believes itself to represent. Whether brought about by election or revolution, governments see themselves as carrying out the policies of the people, but policies such as the redistribution of income or getting Concorde into the air require years or decades for fulfilment. So there is a tendency for governments to take increasing control over their peoples. The most important form of control is propaganda, which is necessary both in democratic and totalitarian countries. Economic policies such as the development of North Sea Oil cannot be stopped just because public opinion changes, yet democratic governments claim to follow public opinion. The only way to resolve this dilemma is for government to manipulate public opinion[1]. And so, whether because of the imperatives of modern technology or of modern political philosophy, the state stretches its tentacles wider and wider over the lives of individuals. This form of collectivism is here to stay.

At the same time, the *individual* has become more important. As feudal and tribal societies break down all over the world, and as urban life becomes more common, so people's horizons are being widened beyond the parochial boundary of the local community or tribe. They become aware of themselves as individuals in a world in which variety and diversity is the norm. Education and literacy provide a person with critical faculties and an awareness that the world is not all like his home patch and that things need not always be as they have been. He begins to disidentify from traditional ways; he begins to experience himself as an individual apart from his own community.

This historical trend was reinforced by the Reformation theologians who thought that the individual was responsible solely to his God and not to the traditions of the church and of medieval society. It was further reinforced by the philosophers during the Renaissance and the Enlightenment who thought of the individual as the basic unit of society. Contrasting with the biblical idea of the individual being complete only in community (Genesis, for example, describes Eve being created since it was not good for man to be alone), a best seller of the Enlightenment was Daniel Defoe's *Robinson Crusoe.* As Emil Brunner puts it[2]:

> 'Robinson Crusoe is the symbol which expresses the philosophy of life prevalent at that time. It is the idea of the self-sufficient individual, to whose existence the coming of a second and third individual does not *essentially* bring anything new. It is the idea of the *contrat social*, which derives the State from the contract concluded by individuals; it is the idea of economic liberalism, which derives the welfare of the community from the egoism of individuals.'

This is perhaps the most influential single idea in western thinking, influential because it corresponds to the increasingly common experience of the person as an island, separated from other people and from the community.

So, yes, the modern state *is* increasingly collectivising the economy; and yes, the person *is* becoming more and more individualised. And these two trends are not unconnected. As suggested in previous chapters, the breakdown of traditional communities has led to what we experience as a two-tier society in which the individual is ranged against collectivity. As the individual freed himself from the local community and its traditions, he found himself controlled by less tangible but no less powerful forces:

> 'The common error was to believe that if the individual were liberated from the smaller groups he would be set free. But in actual fact he was exposed to the influence of mass currents, to the influence of the state, and direct integration into mass society. Finally, he became a victim of propaganda.'[3]

Now that both the concept of the individual and impersonal mass society are in existence, the two feed one another. The excesses of individualism provided the justification for collectivism, while the excesses of collectivism have given plausibility to the arguments of the individualists. For example, the laissez-faire economy of the nineteenth century which exalted the freedom of the individual enabled the powerful to lord it over the weak. Those who were denied earning power, through accident, sickness or old age, went to the wall; the weakest of all, the children of the labouring classes, were exploited ruthlessly. It was to prevent such abuses that the state slowly came to be more and more involved in protecting the weak and providing a safety net of health care and social security below which no one should be allowed to fall. So the welfare state arose to eradicate the abuses of individualism.

But now the welfare state has expanded to such an extent that many believe it to be the main threat to the individual whom it was originally intended to protect. At first the critics of the welfare state tended to be those who were sufficiently well-off to be able to personally afford the benefits offered by the welfare state and who had nothing to lose by its abolition. But now many who definitely are in need of the material provisions of the welfare state are coming to criticise it for dealing with people as cases to be put into bureaucratic boxes rather than as persons with individual needs and rights. Grass-roots organisations such as the Claimants Union and the Mental Patients Union are as much concerned with the rights of individuals as with the quality or quantity of care offered them. Ivan Illich has provided a more intellectual espousal of the right of the individual to determine his own future rather than have his destiny left in the hands of professionals (doctors, social workers, teachers, and so on) employed by the state. So, there has been a swing from the individualism of nineteenth century laissez-faire to the collectivism of the mid-twentieth century paternalistic welfare state and back again to the individualism of late twentieth century self-determination. Each phase reacts to the worst excesses of the previous phase.

This swing is also seen in other areas. It has already been mentioned that the impersonality of the world of politics has led to political apathy and a retreat into private life, especially the private life of the family. As the tax man seems to be taking more and more of the individual's earnings in order to finance this collective behemoth, so the individual is fighting back – the tax fiddle is just one way in which he sees himself protecting his individual earnings from the collective thief. As the state increasingly attempts to control society, so the individual increasingly develops an underworld which is under his own control. In the extreme form of a controlled society such as a prison, a concentration camp, a totalitarian state, or a rationed wartime economy, it is well known that black markets and other ways of getting by are developed by the individual. In minor ways people are engaged every day in much the same operation to protect their individual dignity in our own society.[4]

Not only has the leviathan of the state accentuated the importance to the individual of his own private (under)world. In addition, the actions of countless individuals have helped create this leviathan. The previous chapter on suburbia argued that many of the now intractable problems of the city have been caused in part by the millions of decisions by individuals to move in search of an essentially individualistic suburban dream. We have created a city over which no-one appears to have control because individuals have given up responsibility for society as a whole and because they act regardless of the consequences for others. The traffic between the impersonal political-urban machine and individual apathy is two-way; each is the cause of the other. Here again we see collectivism and individualism, apparently opposed to each other, but in practice thriving on each other. Each has the same fundamental characteristic – it treats the other person, in Martin Buber's terms, not as a unique 'thou' worthy of respect and to whom we are responsible, but as a mass-produced and impersonal 'it' worthy only to be ignored or manipulated. This is the attitude of both individualism and collectivity toward the other person.

This curious parallel between individualism and collectivism, and the way in which they thrive on each other, may also be seen in the fact that a fully planned society or economy requires an e.lite of individuals able to direct and manipulate it: we have a manipulated mass society with individual freedom in jeopardy, which is only possible because of the actions of an elite fully aware of what they are doing and exercising considerable power.

Modern society has thus created a polarisation between society and the individual, and this is reflected in the polarising of the ideologies of individualism and collectivism. This is why there is so much polemic directed from each extreme to the other. The individualist believes the rights of individual freedom to be an absolute good, and the collectivist believes the state, the party, or the class to demand absolute loyalty. But neither the individual nor collectivity are absolutes; rather they are historically produced and man-made categories which modern people have come to believe in as absolutes. In a word, they are idols. A wanderer on the face of the earth, man has found refuge in the individual and in the group.

Like so many idols, they come in pairs – an idol is a false god and so tends not to answer the prayers of its worshippers, who with time become disillusioned and set up an alternative god with what they believe to be opposite characteristics to the first. Disillusion with the god of work leads to the orienting of life toward leisure; disillusion with the city turns people toward the country and to nature; disillusion with the individual leads to collectivism, and disillusion with the state turns us back to the individual. But often it turns out that the new god, far from being the opposite of the first, has much in common with it. As the Preacher said in the Book of Ecclesiastes, there is nothing new under the sun.

Who Are We?

This modern split between the idea that humanity is essentially to be found in the individual and the idea that it is most fully realised in the group, the class, or the race, is at the heart of the modern dilemma – who are we? Just as in the past bitter theological battles were waged over the precise nature of God, so in a humanist era there are doctrinal battles of the nature of man. To say that one believes in man begs the crucial question of who this 'man' is. Modern man has an identity problem.

In an individualistic society, a person gains a sense of identity through uniqueness and individuality. This entails emphasising the differences between myself and others, distinguishing myself from others. In such a society, the aim of a person is to 'distinguish himself': we say with admiration of someone that he looks 'very distinguished' or that 'he has distinguished himself' on the battlefield, in the arts, in his profession, and so on. The conformist is looked down upon, and the person who distinguishes himself from others is admired. In his classic history of the Renaissance, Jacob Burckhardt mentions that this desire for fame came about at the same time as the rise of individualism[5]. For the first time since the Romans and Greeks, the towns of the Renaissance set up lavish memorials to their famous citizens, while painters, writers and sculptors found patrons eager to become immortalised in art. In the middle ages, by contrast, the only people who had been commemorated were saints, and they were memorable not so much for their individuality but for their submission to the will of God and of the church.

If one cannot become famous by doing good deeds, then there is much to be said for achieving notoriety through infamous deeds. Either way one has distinguished oneself from the common stream. Guy Fawkes, Bonnie and Clyde, pirates and highwaymen – all find a place in our hearts and have entered our romantic folklore because we admire them for at least having differentiated themselves from others. The most sophisticated version of this individualism is in the philosophy of existentialism where the most important thing is that the person *acts* – it does not matter so much what he does, so long as he does something. The most newsworthy version is modern vandalism – faced with a future of conformity to a mass-produced society, the young person of today may take the time-honoured path of individualism and distinguish himself by any means from the crowd. If legitimate ways of distinguishing himself are unavilable, then he may choose illegitimate ways; hence the outrageous crime, the 'senseless' mugging, the scrawling of one's name on the faceless walls of the modern city. (It is curious that adults claiming to believe in the individual seem incapable of understanding such traditionally individualistic behaviour; this is explored in chapter 8.)

But distinguishing oneself in more socially acceptable ways also entails costs for others. To distinguish oneself by becoming top dog means that someone else has to be bottom dog; if I am superior then someone else has to be inferior. Sociologists have been much concerned with this phenomenon of status in modern society, and have consistently come to the conclusion that the status system still has the shape of a pyramid with a sharp peak and broad base, although the middle sections appear to be swelling out a little. Status is a zero sum game – I achieve status only by someone else showing deference to me, which reduces his status in equal measure that it increases mine.

This produces a problem. The ideology of individualism says that every person has to distinguish himself if his identity is to remain viable, yet a status system means that there must be as many losers as winners. One way out of this is to identify a group of deviants who are not proper members of society; by pointing the finger at the delinquent, the homosexual or the alcoholic who we believe have forfeited the right to be respected, we can convince ourselves that we ourselves are worthy of respect. By labelling others as bad we know that we are good, by labelling others as mad we know that we must be sane[6]. This righteous indignation, this pointing the finger at him who is bad, enables us to feel good. The same function is played by racial prejudice – here we identify a group, not that has forfeited the right to be counted members of society, but that we believe by birth never had such rights. It is significant that the most racially prejudiced and those with the harshest attitudes toward outsiders such as delinquents and homosexuals are often on the bottom half of the status ladder themselves; society does not accord them much status and so they find it by stigmatising a scapegoat group.

Some find a sense of individual identity by attempting to dominate other members of their family and, significantly, it is in the working class that, traditionally, the man is the boss of the house; accorded no status by society, he finds it through dominating the family. The most insignificant man in the outside world may be a tyrant in his own home. Family members who are the victims of such domination, or who find themselves more subtly engulfed by spouse or parent, may succumb by adopting an ideology that they are the weaker sex and are intended to be dominated. But this fits poorly with the ideology of individualism that all people – American and Russian, male and female – have an individual identity of their own; and so the dominated family member may strive for his or her own identity. But individualism offers the possibility of identity only through distinguishing self from others, which may leave the person with little option other than physical escape from the home (the deserting wife and the runaway daughter) or bizarre behaviour which proclaims that one does after all exist and is to be taken notice of[7].

Finding an identity by distinguishing self from others faces one further hurdle – death. Death is the great leveller. This is less of a problem for the collectivist who finds an identity in tribe, nation, or class, for these things survive the death of the body; but for the individualist, physical death threatens to end identity. With the revival of individualism at the Renaissance, people began to treat death differently[8]. Whereas in the middle ages an unmarked grave near the holy sacrament had been all that was desired, with the advent of modern individualism it became fashionable to have erected a tombstone listing one's earthly achievements for posterity. The walls of the Abbey in Bath, where I live, are choc-a-bloc with verbose plaques exalting the merits of the literati, politicians and businessmen of the English Enlightenment who died and were buried in this fashionable city.

Nowadays, most people are more prosaic about their own death but, because individual identity is generally sustained by marriage rather than by some more enduring social group, many people are peculiarly vulnerable to the death of a spouse, which may have a shattering effect on their sense of unique identity.

The individualist approach to finding an identity therefore results in several acute problems, and an identity constructed on this basis is inherently precarious, because either others or one's own death may topple one's self-assumed superiority. The collectivist approach to constructing an identity is in many ways a good deal simpler, less precarious and less problematic. Here the intention is not to distinguish oneself from the group but to identify with it. Membership of the group is all that is needed to confirm one's sense of self. One is identified as a good Communist, a good Nazi or, less dramatically, a good Englishman, a good boy scout, or a good church member. The concern is not to rise to the top and dominate others, but to be a totally loyal and ordinary member; we thereby ensure that nothing comes between us and the group, and nothing prevents the group identity from attaching to us. The simplicity and universal availability of this kind of identity make it especially attractive to those who are denied status on the individualist ladder.

Fear of standing out from the group produces the conformity that individualist societies criticise in totalitarian ones. The member of the collective is unwilling to criticise the group for fear of splitting it up, since the end of the group means the end of the individual. Soviet dissidents who are hailed in the individualist West for having the courage to stand out from the group, are condemned in the Soviet Union for splitting the solidarity of the Soviet people. Similarly the western espousal of human rights protects personal identity (western style) but is a serious threat to identity (collectivist style).

Standing out from the group is also dangerous because it can lead to excommunication. This is a threat only in a collectivist situation; by contrast, for the individualist to be cast out from the group is not the end of the world since his identity is ultimately bound up in his interior concept of worth rather than in group membership. Excommunication for the Protestant or the Labour Party member is not the tragedy it is for the Catholic or for the Communist Party member in a one-party state.

The role of religion in all this can be mixed. If religion

can be co-opted to support the dominant collectivism (as in Nazi Germany) or the dominant individualism (as in contemporary America) then it is welcomed and manipulated. But a religion which offers a transcendental critique of society in the tradition of the Old Testament prophets, asserts an authority higher than man which puts limits on both the individual and on the collective. It is for fear of this happening that some communist countries are hostile to religion; similarly, existentialism is often loath to form alliances with Christianity. For if the state or the individual are not God, then the very foundations of collectivism and individualism have been challenged. For the collectivist, the state must not be challenged by either individual members or by religion; for the individualist, the individual must not be challenged by either the state or by religion. As soon as such a challenge takes hold, then the very basis on which personal identity has been constructed is also challenged, and people can be very resentful of this.

So individualism and collectivism, far from being simply abstract notions of importance only to politicians and philosophers, have profound implications for our very notion of self, of who we are. The way I look at my behaviour is fundamentally different in the two philosophies. Collectivism identifies people with their behaviour. Thus in a communist society, because I see myself in terms of a loyal party member, my work in a factory for the benefit of the state is a true embodiment of myself. In individualism, by contrast, there is a fundamental alienation between self and behaviour; I disidentify from my boring mundane activities by believing in an underlying 'real me' that is altogether more masculine, romantic, in control, and so on. The most profound alienation is perhaps felt by the individualist living, like a fish out of water, in a collectivist society, for there is virtually no behaviour with which he can identify.

It was mentioned in the chapter on the family that people tend to assess social institutions on whether they benefit individual development or society as a whole. It is not just feelings about the family that are split along these lines. International disagreement over human rights faces the same problem; and the debate on law and order, on whether offenders should be treated for their own good or to protect society, is similarly grounded. This polarisation between the individual and society is a historically-rooted gulf that is now so deep that it has become almost a paradigm for discussion about social problems. It is because debates on the family, on human rights, and on law and order are based on two opposing sacreds to which combatants give their ultimate allegiance that it is most unlikely that such debates will ever be resolved within society as it is now known.

Identity and Salvation

The contemporary search for identity may be seen as a de-Christianised version of the religious search for salvation. Seen in this light, some interesting similarities emerge. Two of the recurrent heresies that Christians have succumbed to in the search for salvation correspond to the modern modes of seeking an identity. One is that salvation may be obtained by good works, by doing good deeds that show one is better than others and therefore worthy of salvation. This finds an echo in the modern notion that identity is to be found by distinguishing oneself from others, by showing oneself to be superior. Both the ancient and modern versions of this salvation-identity by works tend to produce anxiety and neuroticism in the individual for he has to constantly strive to attain a salvation or identity that is always precarious. There is always the possibility that he may lose that salvation through future neglect or that others may overtake him.

The other heresy is that salvation derives simply from being a member of the church, by being born or baptised into it. This finds a modern echo in achieving identity through belonging to the group, a method that is much less anxiety-provoking, but carries the dangers of dependence on church or group and therefore liability to being exploited. This is indeed what happened in the abuses of medieval Catholicism.

According to the mainstream of biblical Christianity,

though, salvation is found neither by good works nor through membership of the church, but is a gift freely and directly received from God. This frees us from dependence both on personal achievements and on being accepted by the group. Within this traditional formulation of salvation there may lie a clue to the transcending of the modern worship of the achievements of the individual and the worship of the state. Let's examine this with reference to the idolatry of the individual and of his personal achievements.

There is a sense in which the attempt to find oneself by distinguishing oneself from others is doomed to failure. It involves aiming at an ideal self which I would like to be, and this ideal, however freely chosen, is always chosen from the stock of ideals lying around in society. Any ideal I choose is therefore conformist, and I end up aiming at some version of what society says I ought to want to be. The most ambitious is in some ways the most predictable. So even if I attain my ideal, I have still not found my individual self, but merely attained some kind of conformity with society. Aiming at the ultimate in individuality, I have become a product of that society.

This was perhaps most succinctly put by Jesus when he said that 'by gaining his life a man will lose it; by losing his life for my sake, he will gain it' (Matthew 10.39). By trying to find my self I will surely not find it; but by letting go of self for the sake of others I will paradoxically find my true self. The person who abandons all conceptions and ambitions of the kind of person he would like to be and begins living for others (and the Christian would add, for God) finds himself growing through all the unexpected things which come his way. If the person is living for others (or for God), there is no telling where this will lead and his life will become truly unique, truly distinguished from the ordinary. This is the paradox of love: to love means to give of myself, to diminish myself. It means to orient self to the needs of the other, rather than to my own needs and wants, and so it involves a diminishing of my own individuality for the sake of another, for the sake of community. Yet it is the human experience that when we love like this, we find true kinship not only with others but also with our own self.

Both individualism and collectivism treat other people as means to an end, as an 'it' to be used rather than as a unique 'thou'. It is only with the rediscovery of the other as 'thou' that we will be able to abolish the modern dichotomy between the individual and society. In love (which includes more than sexual and family love) the two become one, and a real unity between fellow humans becomes possible just at that moment that the individual relinquishes selfhood. As Brunner put it[9]:

> 'The relation between the individual and the community is not a philosophical but a theological problem. To the Christian faith both these ideas – the 'individual' and the 'community' – appear to be untrue, and sinful. No adjustment between the two is possible, for it is impossible to make one 'good' out of two kinds of sin. In the Christian faith the individual is so defined that he cannot be imagined apart from the community. . . . The individual as such does not and cannot exist at all, the very *conception* of the individual implies and includes that of the community.'

In other words, the true individual and true community exist only in and through the exercise of love.

But loving others is not possible unless I am myself loved. Only then will I feel a secure sense of worth, of being valued, so that I can go out and relate to others without needing them to confirm my sense of worth. Only then will I have lost my need to dominate others and elicit deference from them. Only then will I be free to relate to others, for only then will I have ceased to need them for my own ends. To say this is, of course, no more than teaching one's grandmother to suck eggs, since the good parent for example knows that it is only the child who is unconditionally loved that grows up with the sense of self-worth that enables it to relate to others in a non-manipulative way. It is also the discovery that so excited Martin Luther and the early Protestant reformers when they began to experience the freedom that derives from the knowledge of being unconditionally loved by God.

This receiving of unconditional love brings us back to where we began this modest theological excursion, to *grace*. Salvation, bringing with it a renewed sense of worth, is not something to be individually striven for or attained by conformity to the group, but is freely given by God. Here is unconditional love of the kind that is essential if the dichotomy of the individual and society, of self and others, is to be transcended. The vision of a society built on overflowing grace instead of on the present futile struggle to achieve a home for ourselves is one of the main motives behind this book.

6
At Home Among the Animals – The Ecology Movement

In Search of a New Religion

Idolatry, the ascribing of absolute worth to things and persons, seems universal among human beings. Believing in the value of some thing, person or cause, gives direction to life and the chaos of existence acquires some semblance of order. The sacred provides mankind the wanderer with a home base. The historical process usually called secularisation does not involve a shift from belief to non-belief, but a shift in what is believed in. If people no longer believe in God, there are perhaps two other broad alternatives for belief: belief in Man, and belief in Nature. If people will not worship the Creator, they will worship the creature or creation.

Faith in Man (humanism) has been the dominant faith of modern industrial society. Although the Man that is believed in varies widely, from the individual of bourgeois capitalism to the proletarian class of orthodox Marxism, there have been certain elements that modern humanism has consistently held to. For example, in both East and West it is presumed that human beings are rational and naturally good, that the aim of life is happiness, and that human history is a continual progress[1].

These notions have taken a battering of late, though. The emergence of the nuclear threat put a question mark over the idea that history would develop endlessly; history could come instead to a dramatic and final full stop in a nuclear holocaust. Perhaps one reason why the British Campaign for Nuclear Disarmament of the 1950s and 60s found such strong support among articulate humanists was that nuclear war challenged this fundamental tenet of humanism. More recently, the worldwide economic crisis of the 1970s and the increasing scarcity of raw materials and of energy is raising doubts as to whether economic progress can be sustained indefinitely. The presumption that human beings are rational and good took a severe beating with the Vietnam War, for here was the most civilised and expensively educated nation on earth putting enormous resources into a barbarous war which it could not hope to win. Social problems, slums, racial riots, and widespread starvation have made people wonder whether the result of civilisation and industry is happiness, or whether there is perhaps as much misery in the world as ever.

The confident 1950s in which it was widely believed that mankind could build a new world out of the ashes of World War Two gave way to the turmoil and puzzlement of the 60s in which this dream seemed to fade and was rejected by many of the new generation; this in turn has led to the apathetic 70s in which both the optimism of the 50s and the disillusion of the 60s have become blurred, and western nations drift along from one economic or political 'crisis' to the next. Humanism believed that man shaped his own future, and both optimists and rebels of earlier decades believed this, but this has been replaced by a feeling that one must take life as it comes and muddle through.

Humanism has lost much of its plausibility; in the early 60s, it was all the rage among young intellectuals, but is not so fashionable now. So, if God is dead and Man is in disgrace, an obvious candidate for worship is Nature. Alongside disillusion with man-made things such as cities, political institutions and technology, there has arisen faith in natural things. Natural materials fill the blossoming craft shops, natural childbirth is coming back into fashion, natural scenery is drawing tourists back to those remoter rural areas vacated by their agricultural forebears[2].

Even in academic life, Nature is staging a comeback. Until the last decade or so the dominant idea in psychology was that human behaviour was largely learned (something over which we had control and which illustrated our sophistication over other species), but now there is increasing interest in the idea that the human personality develops similarly to the physical maturation of the body. In linguistics, Noam Chomsky argues that the acquisition by the individual of language develops naturally as much as being learned. Wilson's *Sociobiology* (1975) which argues that culture is biologically derived has been received sympathetically, in stark contrast to the howls of abuse that Jensen received in 1968 when he argued that IQ is largely inherited. Desmond Morris's books such as *The Naked Ape* are best sellers, and there is renewed interest in ethology, a discipline which studies both animal and human social organisation within the same theoretical framework. Overall, it has become fashionable to look to biology and to nature in order to understand human society and human behaviour.

Feeling somewhat homeless and ill at ease in the world man has created, many people are turning to the world of nature. Of course, just as belief in Man or God can mean many different things to suit the convenience of the age, so can belief in Nature. Nature can be red in tooth and claw, or it can be Mother Nature, the Earth Goddess that brings peace and security; Nature can be denigrated as the seat of all earthly passions and therefore to be repressed, or it can be exalted as the source of instinctual spontaneity and freedom. So, the mere fact that people are rediscovering nature does not tell us very much; what we need to know is, what kind of nature are they turning to?

Clearly if nature is to provide us with a new home and a sense of identity, then certain ideas about it are more appealing than others: *evolution*, for example. Over the last century or so, many have been keen to draw the conclusion that man is the peak of evolution and is therefore top dog on this planet. In the past this notion appealed to humanists and, after a little rethinking, to Christians also, for both believe mankind to be special in some way. But with the decline of both the humanist and the Christian world view, human nobility and superiority have come into question, and evolution does not have quite the powerful appeal of old.

Instead the approach to nature that is currently enjoying popularity is that of *ecology*. The 'ecology movement' is one of the more publicised phenomena of the late 1960s and 1970s, although there is in fact more than one such movement, and they do not all agree. Nevertheless, the fact that an ecology movement is believed to exist indicates that it is becoming recognised as an idea of some importance. (Academic ecologists may disavow much of what the popularisers say, and this is an occupational hazard of academics whose subject suddenly comes into the limelight. This chapter, though, is restricted to *popular* ecology.)

Popular ecology portrays nature as a harmonious system of different parts, one of which is man. Man thus has a rather humbler role than in the evolutionary model, a role which fits the blunted aspirations of the times. But it is not a negligible role, for we are entrusted with stewardship of the earth; we must respect nature and abide by its laws, but the proper functioning of Planet Earth depends on exercise of human responsibility. Ecology demotes us from being masters over nature, but leaves us with the not inconsiderable post of chief steward.

Ecosystems are said to operate according to natural laws and, as man is an animal like the rest, our social systems when functioning properly operate according to the same laws. One law is that 'all ecosystems tend toward stability . . . the more diverse and complex the ecosystem the more stable it is'[3]. This idea of nature and, by implication, society as consisting of stable and ordered systems with everything happily in its right place is a great attraction and comfort to those who feel homeless and at risk in the modern world. It reassures them that this disintegration of society is not natural and that the application of a little reason and science can restore order and harmony. This extrapolation from ecological to social systems is explicitly made by some writers; Murray Bookchin, for example, talks of this particular ecological law as a 'reconstructive credo for a humanistic society', just what we need if we are to rebuild the world now that both God and Man are dead[4]. (Strictly academic ecologists, by contrast, are rather more reticent about proclaiming their findings as universal laws.)

What Bookchin and company are advocating is not dissimilar from the nineteenth-century idea that society is like a biological organism with different parts all functioning to sustain the whole. One of the beauties of this idea, like any idea derived from science, is that it may be used to justify any social and political arrangement one desires. The organism model, for example, was often used to justify the status quo: if a social institution existed then it must perform some valuable function for society as a whole and should therefore be maintained. Bookchin uses the modern ecological variant of this model to advance an anarchism remarkably similar to Victorian laissez-faire: if the constituent parts naturally lead to a harmonious whole then there is no need for controls and constraints within society for these are unnatural and the cause of instability; it is only when rules and constraints are removed that the parts will be able to function normally and a stable society be restored.

Philosophically speaking, this deriving of moral lessons and political programmes from nature is dubious; it commits the naturalistic fallacy of attempting to derive an 'ought' from an 'is'. But logic aside, it is a very convenient trick. With religion and humanism both in disgrace, modern societies face the problem of what sociologists call 'legitimation' – where to get a set of ideas that can justify our social institutions and way of life, where to find a rationale that will keep people happy with their lot. One time-honoured legitimation is Nature – people believe that all kinds of things are 'natural' and therefore not only inevitable but also legitimate. Thus, 'It's *natural* for the mother to look after the pre-school child' (even though there is no school, and therefore no pre-school, in nature). 'It's *natural* to want to get on in life' (even though there are many societies in which ambition is just as naturally disapproved of) – and so on. Until the last few years this invoking of nature to justify social norms has relied on 'common sense'. What popular ecology writers have done is to link the age-old legitimation of Nature with the modern legitimation of Science (modern man believes that if something is scientific, or has been discovered by science, then it must be true and right). The new ecological moralisers claim that if mankind follows the laws of ecology then we are being both natural and scientific, which together produces the most powerful rationale going today.

So the ecological view of Nature provides a new home for rootless, modern man. It gives us a location in the universe which fits the somewhat jaded contemporary mood, it assures us that social harmony is possible even in a complex modern society, and it provides a rationale that will justify anything and everything.

But it is not just a home that popular versions of ecology provide us with. They also provide a way of coping with the peculiarly modern twist to death and suffering. The previous chapter noted that one of the problems of individualism is that physical death brings with it social death; the person does not live on as in a tribe or ancestor cult. Rather than identifying with an enduring social group such as the tribe, or in modern collectivist societies the nation or party, the individual's sense of identity is bound up with spouse and children and is therefore peculiarly mortal. It is interesting that one of the key words of the modern ecology movement(s) is *survival*, and that perhaps the best known book of popular ecology is *A Blueprint for Survival*. Ecology is not talking about the survival of the individual; it is the survival of the species, of mankind on this earth. By stressing this, modern individualistic man is encouraged to identify with the whole human species. Once this identification has been achieved, then the problem of mortality becomes amenable to scientific management, for the popularisers claim the science of ecology holds the key to survival of the species. The importance of this re-identification if we are to survive is stressed by Kenneth Boulding, one of the leading lights of the ecology movement in America. Conservationists are apt to appeal to our sense of responsibility to posterity, but Boulding comments that:

'It is always a little hard to find a convincing answer

> to the man who says 'what has posterity ever done for me?' . . . The only answer to this . . . is to point out that the welfare of the individual depends on the extent to which he can identify himself with others, and that the most satisfactory individual identity is that which identifies not only with a community in space but also with a community extending over time from the past into the future.'[5]

In passing, it is worth noting that justifying present conservation in terms of responsibility to future generations and to mankind as a whole conveniently sidesteps the crucial consideration that man is pitted against man and that what is in the interest of one group of people (say, the West) may not be in the interests of another (say, the Third World). 'Posterity' thus provides a legitimation as well as immortality; it enables me to pull the wool over the eyes of others and foist my sectional interests on the whole world. To advocate responsibility to posterity, or to mankind, muddies the issue – to whom, precisely, are we being responsible? It cloaks self-interestedness under a rhetoric of responsibility and altruism. It is considerably more devious than the traditional notion of responsibility to God, in which it can be spelt out clearly what God we are talking about.

'Survival', like the rest of the ecological view of Nature, fits the mood of the times. The exaltation of the survival of the species as the prime value to which politicians as well as ecologists should gear themselves implies that there are no higher values, that there is nothing worth dying for. As Richard Neuhaus has commented, this seems to have lost sight of Jesus' insight that by seeking life we will not find it, that only by seeking after other values will we end up with life: if there is nothing worth dying for, then there is nothing worth living for either. Indeed, there is evidence from Hiroshima that those who do survive a holocaust, even if only by good fortune, feel lifelong guilt that they survived and others perished[6]. So survival seems dubious as an ultimate value on both theological and psychological grounds, but it does fit the contemporary mood. Its implication that there is nothing worth dying for rings deep emotional bells with those living in a post-Vietnam America and an apathetic Britain. Quite what we would want to survive for, ecology cannot tell us (indeed, evolution says that sooner or later all species become extinct in the onward march of evolution, and ecology adds that we are merely a species like the rest), but that does not bother many members of modern society. Deeply sceptical of political ideologies and of traditional religion, they prefer to be left alone to enjoy the benefits of a consumer society rather than seek the purpose of existence. Survival for no purpose is what modern society is largely about, and ecology reflects this.

It was mentioned in chapter 1 that, in addition to the problems of homelessness and mortality, a peculiarly poignant modern problem is *suffering*. Ecology can ease the pain of this, or at least provide a rationale for suffering. By focusing attention at the level of the ecosystem (and by implication the social system) instead of the individual components (e.g. people) of such systems, it reduces the importance of the individual member of society. The needs of the individual are subordinated to the need of the human race for survival. Thus the suffering or even death of individuals may be necessary for the sake of the whole race; indeed, this sacrifice of individuals for the sake of the species is happening all the time in nature. The ecology movement has not stressed this point to date, but the groundwork has been laid for a rather insidious development, the idea that some people will have to be sacrificed for the rest of us. Because ecology is a brainchild of the affluent West, it is meeting resistance in many poor countries (why *should* they control their populations just because we are frightened of being outnumbered, why *should* they conserve their raw materials just because we are worried our industrial machine will collapse?), and it is clear that if anyone is to be sacrificed it will not be us but them. Lest the use of ecology to justify this kind of suffering sound unlikely, it is worth remembering that the evolutionary idea of the survival of the fittest was abused by both nineteenth-century laissez-faire and by twentieth century fascism to justify the exploitation or extermination of the politically and economically weak.

The strength of any popular movement derives not from the logic or truth of its ideas, but from whether it meets some social, psychological or economic need within society. The theme of this book is that mankind needs social institutions and ideas that provide a sense of being at home in the world, a sense of immortality, a rationale for suffering and a means of coming to terms with nature. It is the scarcity of these cultural resources, as much as of physical resources such as oil and food, that gives ecology its contemporary plausibility.

Masters or Slaves?

The predominant attitude of western culture toward nature over the past four hundred years has been that man is the master of nature, able to exploit it for his own ends. One of the reasons that ecology is finding such a willing audience today is that this traditional notion of mastery over nature is becoming a little implausible. The more we seem to bridle nature and lead it by the reins, the more nature is inclined to take a kick back at us. Pollution is on the increase, the shortage of energy and raw materials suggests that nature can impose limits on human beings, and the levelling out of human life expectancy in the developed world suggests that there are limits to what modern technology and medicine can achieve. The more horrendous estimates that we are irrevocably polluting the oceans and have committed ourselves to a level of economic growth which sooner or later can only destroy us[7], if true, mean that in the long run it is nature who will be our master and we its slave.

Of course, throughout the industrial revolution the lower classes understood the human and environmental costs of the exploitation of nature. Living downwind from smoky factories, they knew all about the pollution, the environmental hazards and the increased mortality that 'mastery' over nature involved. But it has not been until recently that pollution and the like have built up to the extent that they have also affected the middle and upper classes, the opinion makers. Smog spreads to the suburbs, the salmon die in the high-class rivers, and suddenly pollution is announced as the new worldwide crisis. Human exploitation of nature has always involved human beings exploiting other human beings; now though the boot is on the other foot. We are all beginning to feel the costs of exploitation, and so the very idea of man having the right to exploit nature is coming under criticism.

This is an oversimplification, however. It is not just that once we believed ourselves to be masters and now we are wondering whether we are becoming the slaves of nature. Actually, western culture has always been somewhat ambivalent about man's relation to nature. True, industry has tended to extract the last ounce from nature just as, in the search for profit, it has tried to extract the last ounce from its human workers. But scientists have had a rather more respectful view of nature. It has often been argued that modern science began when a Protestant biblical view came to replace the Catholic-medieval worldview in the seventeeth century. In the medieval view, the material world of Nature occupied an inferior position to the spiritual world of Grace and was not believed worthy of man's highest endeavours and talents. But the Reformation released the natural world as an arena given by God to man for his benefit, and so work became more highly rated (chapter 2) and the scientific study of the natural world became a fit occupation for human minds[8]. Thus science began with the notion that nature operated with God-given laws; the laws of nature were to be respected, because God-given, and the task of science was to discover these laws. If man was to improve his material lot, it was not by trampling over the laws of nature, but by discovering them and harnessing them to his service. With time, this religious basis of science became less relevant, but respect for nature was still maintained, especially since scientists had now come to see man himself as operating according to natural laws. And even today when the notion of scientific 'laws' to be 'discovered' is rather dubious philosophically, scientists have not lost their amazement at the throne of nature.

Historically then, our rather ambiguous relation to nature has been expressed largely by business and industry taking the stance that man is master of nature, and science taking the other stance that man is part of nature and has ultimately to bow before its majesty. Now that the ill effects of industrialisation are catching up with us, its critics are tending to lump science and Christianity along with industry as the baddies who have fouled up the environment. And there is some justification in this, since both Christianity and science have been invaluable lackeys of industry. Popular ecology has often asserted that industry, science and Christianity have been united in a view of man as the master of nature, that this view is the root of all our present pollution woes, and that therefore the way forward is to relocate man as an integral part of nature.

According to ecologists, the problem started with the idea that man and nature are distinct entities. Here Christianity is often blamed because, along with Judaism, it clearly stated that God, man and nature were separate entities, whereas in most other religions they tend to be fused together. Once we had ceased to identify with nature, the way was open for us to exploit nature ruthlessly, for by hurting nature we were no longer hurting ourselves[9]. As Aldous Huxley expresses it:

> 'Committing that sin of overweening bumptiousness which the Greeks called hubris, we behave as though we were not members of earth's ecological community, as though we were privileged and, in some sort, supernatural beings and could throw our weight around like Gods.'[10]

Others argue that, Christian or not, 'civilised' man has always acted in this spirit of arrogance. This is the reason, according to one book[11], for the rise and fall of all the great civilisations, and ours will be no exception:

> 'Civilised man nearly always was able to become master of his environment temporarily. His chief troubles came from his delusions that his temporary mastership was permanent. He thought of himself as 'master of the world', while failing to understand fully the laws of nature. . . . When he tries to circumvent the laws of

> nature, he usually destroys the natural environment that sustains him. And when his environment deteriorates rapidly, his civilisation declines.'

The ecological blueprint for human survival then, says that we should abolish the idea of a dichotomy between ourselves and nature, that we should respect the laws of nature and live in harmony with them. From the slogans stitched onto jeans inviting us to 'Be Natural' to the lengthy polemics of the ecologists, the message is the same: the way forward is for man to identify unambiguously with nature.

Is this possible? The relation of man to nature is inherently ambiguous in that man is both creature and creator. It turns out that popular ecology, while claiming to identify unambiguously with nature, is in fact as ambiguous as everything else. Popular ecologists cite animal studies; for example, overcrowding in rats is used to argue that man should control his own population or else nasty things will happen. As we are part of nature, it is said, we should learn from scientific studies of nature; but these very studies examine non-human systems; that is, they assume nature to consist of everything *other* than man. As soon as man is unequivocally placed within nature, then the logic of the argument breaks down. This constant slipping of man in and out of nature is well illustrated in the following extract from a book which introduces ecology to the layman (comments in italics are added):

> 'Man is an animal and as such can be viewed in an ecological context. But man is unusual in that he utilises a far greater proportion of the world's resources than any other animal. (*Man = part of nature*). . . .
> Many of man's activities are destructive of nature (*Nature being everything other than man*). . . .
> It therefore becomes essential that we examine ourselves from an ecological point of view and try to place ourselves in a framework which is part of nature; (*Man = part of nature*)
> but this is not possible until we understand how the natural world operates'. (*The natural world being everything other than man*)[12]

Indeed, ecologists have actually increased the dichotomy between man and nature by emphasising that we should try to understand nature and its ecological laws:

> 'If it is possible for man to comprehend and so exercise power over the system of which he is nominally part, then he has externalised it. A distinction is being made between man the comprehender and that which is comprehended. No matter how strenuously he may deny it, the ecologist bases the whole of his argument on this dualism.'[13]

A metaphor which ecology has often used is that of 'Spaceship Earth' – we and the other species are all together on this planet spinning through space and somehow or other we have to get along together. This metaphor is supposed to illustrate the identity of interests between man and other species. But it turns out that this metaphor, far from being nature-oriented, is about the most man-centred metaphor that could be devised. One ecologically-minded commentator has seen the problem here:

> 'A spaceship is completely a human artifact designed to sustain human life and no other purpose. . . . The spaceship mentality is the final sophistication of this disastrous man-centred view of the nature of things and the things of nature, and it has the present allurement of seeming to offer ecologic solutions without sacrifice of the old presuppositions.'[14]

Precisely at the point of claiming to be nature-oriented, the old man-centred view creeps back in.

To sum up, ecology's claim to place man firmly within nature is a great attraction in a post-Christian, post-humanist age because it provides a sense of home, of having a place in the scheme of things. But any solution (ecological or otherwise) to the problem of homelessness that denies the religious nature of the problem is misplaced. It provides an insecure home, and to see the impossibility of consistently maintaining that man is purely part of nature one has to go no further than the writings of ecologists themselves. It is as false as the idol it replaces

– the arrogant idea of autonomous man, the master of nature.

The age-old problem of our relation to nature is one of the fundamental dilemmas of mankind, and one of the major tasks of human cultures is to enable people to come to terms with this dilemma (chapter 1). The solutions to the dilemma, that were so important a part of industrial society over the last couple of hundred years are now creaking at the seams, and one of the attractions of ecology is that it offers a new framework for integrating man and nature. But as this framework tries to deny the ambiguity of man as both creature and creator, as both part of and apart from nature, it ends up contradicting itself and smuggling back the old idea of man the master. So long as this hidden face of ecology remains hidden, ecology will continue to be attractive, for it will continue to offer the appearance of a radical solution; and with the problems of pollution, population increase and so on being of the magnitude they are, people want radical solutions. Or at least solutions that appear radical.

Cut-Price Radicalism

It is not just in its view of nature that popular ecology tries to be radical. Its whole rhetorical style depends on its claim to offer radical alternatives to conventional modes of thought that have been or will be the downfall of industrial society. Typical ecological rhetoric is of the following kind:

1. *Western civilisation is committed to X*, e.g. limitless growth, a technological solution to all problems, arrogance vis-a-vis nature, the large scale.
2. *X is having disastrous consequences*, e.g. the exhaustion of natural resources, starvation, pollution.
3. *Therefore what is needed is Y (Y being the opposite of X)*, e.g. limits to growth, a new set of values to replace the old faith in technology, humility before nature, small is beautiful.
4. *Examples of Y are to be found in Z (where Z is*

somewhere other than modern industrial society), e.g. the Ancient East, hunter-gatherer tribes, and of course Nature.

This rhetoric has the appearance of being radical, of digging down to the core of modern society and finding it rotten. But as with its assertions about nature, the rhetoric very often implicitly assumes the very modes of thought that it explicitly condemns. Y often turns out not to be the opposite of X, but simply X disguised in new clothing. For example: the rejection of the arrogant idea that man can control nature turns out to entail an even greater arrogance – that man can control himself and can invent a brand new future. This is exactly the kind of optimistic humanism that motivated planners and politicians after 1945 and which was so thoroughly discredited in the 1960s. Consider technology: ecology says that we should no longer put our faith in technology, but then proceeds to enthuse about small-scale technology (a windmill for everyone) with a passion that exceeds that of conventional engineers. Popular ecology rejects technological tinkering with nature as the solution to our problems, and then proposes using the modern technology of birth control to tinker with natural human fertility in an attempt to control the population explosion. It claims to reject the large-scale and proclaims that small is beautiful; yet the number of professional ecologists that would be needed to run the new utopia is mind-boggling, and would bring organisational problems as big as any that big business knows today.

It would be unfair to say that popular ecology engages in this kind of double-talk in every sentence it utters; indeed, some of these criticisms have come from ecologists themselves. Nevertheless, this substanceless rhetoric is characteristic. While claiming to be radical, the ecology movement is imbued with the premises of the humanism that is at the heart of the industrial society it tries to criticise. These premises were outlined at the beginning of this chapter. *First, that man is rational.* The frequent rhetoric about the science of ecology as the ethical base for a reconstructed society indicates that reason and science are as important to the critics as to those being criticised. And just as humanism saw 'the facts' as the main weapon in demolishing the 'naive beliefs' of religion, so the 'facts' and 'laws' discovered by ecology are now being used to demolish the technocrats' naive hope in technology. 'Hope rather than fact is basic to many of their assertions', accuses one ecologist[16].

Second, the premise that man is naturally good. Ecology assumes this too, for there would be little point calling man to repent for his ecological sins were he not capable of turning around from his errors. The polluters are often portrayed as a small depraved minority, and if only the majority of people were true to their own nature and properly educated then all would be well.

Third, the assumption that history is a matter of continual progress, that what is new is good. This too ecology subtly affirms. Why else would it cover up the conventionality of its ideas if not to give the impression that, for the west at least, they are totally new and radical? Ecology thus cashes in on the modern belief that what is new is best and what is radical is true.

The ecology movement offers cut-price radicalism, the feel of being radical without seriously challenging the premises of modern humanism. This is just what some people want, and to see why, we need to go back yet again to the problem of homelessness. The ecology movement is largely supported by people from the middle classes of western societies, and this group is undergoing a disturbing upheaval in its view of the world. With the rise in raw material prices, inflation, white-collar unemployment, the bottom falling out of the myth of progress, the new insecurity of the professions, an increasing sense of powerlessness and the rebellion of their young, the world of the middle classes is manifestly precarious. (The working class, by contrast, has always borne the brunt of unemployment and powerlessness, is traditionally sceptical about progress, and on the whole it is not working-class children who are rebelling.) The middle classes need a new social order, a new view of the world, a world in which they can feel more at home. Such a world must appear new and radical enough to convince them it can cope with an age of change, but at the same time it must give off deeply reassuring vibrations; after all, they do not want a revolution. It is exactly this subtle combination of radical rhetoric and conventional wisdom that the ecology movement offers. What is on offer is a package deal in which people can believe they are creating a whole new world, while in practice continuing with the familiar old one. Ecology provides hope at no cost.

One section of the middle class is particularly in need of this package deal. This is the generation that participated in the counter-culture and the student revolution of the late 1960s and found by the early 70s that utopia had not arrived. Here is a generation that had invested much, both emotionally and in terms of careers and life-style, in being rebels, but it is now more or less disillusioned. As family life and inflation force them back into the career market, perhaps they wish to return to the middle-class fold whence they originally came, yet they cannot lose face by becoming overtly conformist. To this group, the environmentalist movement comes as a godsend for it allows them to articulate a thoroughly conventional world view with all the appearance of the most thorough-going radicalism. The liberal has been caricatured as 'a communist with a wife and two kids'; perhaps the environmentalist is a hippy with a wife and two kids.

I believe it is right that we try to rethink our relation to the environment and join in the search for an environmental ethic. But the strength and the plausibility of the ecology movement does not depend on the scientists, philosophers or theologians coming up with intellectually valid answers. While the experts argue, the ordinary conservationist digging away to restore a river bank accepts ecology as a package deal, contradictions and all, and it is precisely this contradictory package of radicalism and conventionality which gives him a warm reassurance that perhaps he can find a home in the world after all.

7
Culture as Sacred: Race and Relativism

A major theme of this book is that human cultures enable people to maintain a sense of having a place in an ordered world. Without the embrace of culturally accepted values, customs and habits, life would disintegrate into the void of absurdity; without the structure that society provides for everyday activity and the limits it imposes on our thinking, everything would become shifting sand. Thus human beings conspire through culture to cover up their state of homelessness in the universe.

Different societies create different cultures, and the (largely middle-class) Anglo-American culture described in this book, with its emphasis on work, the small isolated family, individualism, and recently an interest in Nature, is only one of an unknown number of cultures that have been constructed over thousands of years.

Race

In these two facts – the function of culture in providing a sense of security, and the diversity of cultures – are the seeds of a problem. For if a society is to feel secure then its culture needs to be all-embracing; people need to believe that their own culture provides the only right and proper way of doing things; they need to know that the way they do things is not just the way their society has always done things but that it is also the right way of doing things. Awareness of the existence of other cultures with different norms, values and customs threatens the monopoly of one's culture in the bid for one's allegiance, for perceiving other ways of doing things raises the possibility that one's own way may not be the best way. Most cultures have had to face this problem, since very few have been so isolated as to have had no contact with other peoples. Even in the simplest cultures in the most sparsely populated regions, there has generally been contact with other cultures through trade, war or in folklore.

Most societies cope with such contact by interpreting other societies so that their own traditional ways are not challenged. Some of the most striking examples of this came in the first contacts between European explorers and native peoples. The natives, never before having seen a white man, a square-rigged sailing ship or an aeroplane, found ways of making sense of these strange new things in terms of their traditional ways of thought. The white man, for instance, might be seen as some kind of god. The Europeans for their part did much the same, interpreting the strange things they found into their own thought forms; for example, the first discoveries of tribes who quite happily went about naked animated theological discussions about whether such and such a place was in fact the Garden of Eden, while cannibals were sometimes thought not to be human at all but animals. The accounts of explorers were often cited in debates about the evolution of man, with the most recently discovered tribe regularly being believed to be the most primitive and therefore of key evolutionary significance. Newly discovered tribes were always seen through particular theological and scientific spectacles[1].

The first contacts between Europeans and other cultures were often fleeting. A ship would stop at an island to get fresh water and provisions and soon sail on; such infrequent contact often constituted a honeymoon period in European/native relations. Neither needed much from the other that could not be given, and relations could be quite amicable, even though based on gross mutual misunderstanding. Each side tended to romanticise the other, and on the European side, myths like that of the noble savage flourished. At such a distance, it was possible to enjoy and appreciate the 'curiosities' of native life; present day logs of expeditions to the Amazon jungle or the odd comments about Sherpa life that sprinkle the books of Himalayan mountaineers reflect a similar fascination with local life.

This honeymoon period in exploration was generally short-lived. As the initial explorers temporarily visiting a new land were succeeded by permanent settlers, cultural differences were no longer a matter for disinterested fascination. The settlers either needed the locals cleared off the land or, later, wanted them as a cheap labour force. The traditional land rights and cultural customs of the locals were ruthlessly steamrollered out of existence by European concepts of land ownership, property, government and law. (For their part, native peoples soon lost their illusions about the white man being some kind of god and came to see him either as a human enemy to be fought or as a human master.) The American Red Indians, for example, were seen by the first settlers in the seventeenth century as amicable souls, then in the nineteenth as enemies to be exterminated, and in the twentieth as a subdued people utterly dependent on their white political overlords. Now their culture has been almost entirely wiped out, it is possible to romanticise them once again. The motto 'the only good Indian is a dead Indian' has now taken on a new meaning, for once Indian culture is dead it is no longer a threat to western economic development, and a romantic view can re-emerge for the first time since the days of the very earliest explorers.

Economic and political greed has been a major reason why colonial powers have, over the last 400 years, flattened the majority of human cultures. A worldwide scientific/economic/Christian/western culture has been substituted which re-interprets any remaining local cultures into the scientific category of 'primitive', the economic category of 'underdeveloped' or (in earlier years) the Christian category of 'pagan'. All cultures are judged according to a western view of social evolution, economic progress and Christian salvation; any culture other than that of western capitalism is believed to be inferior, and the moral supremacy of western culture is thereby protected.

But it is not just political and economic greed that has led to this attitude to other cultures. Certainly economic self-interest helps explain white South Africa's denial of equal status to the black majority, but it does not explain the equally appalling treatment of the aborigine by white Australia. The aborigines make up only about 1% of the population of the Australian continent and so, unlike in South Africa, it would cost the white man virtually nothing to give the aborigine his full rights (although certainly there are economic conflicts between aboriginal land rights and the intentions of white companies to extract uranium and other minerals).

What is involved in addition to economic greed, is the difficulty people have in living next door to another, totally different culture. It is altogether too threatening to realise that one's own way of life is not God-given and sacrosanct, and that one's country and its institutions may not be God's sole gift to mankind. 'One of man's greatest inner needs is to feel that he is right', says Ellul[2]. This need for righteousness appears to be universal, and anthropologists have found that all societies are ethnocentric – they all believe their own way of life to be right and proper and best. People of a different culture, if they come too close, threaten our sense of an undisputed position in the world.

This is particularly a problem for the British in a post-colonial era. All kinds of people may pose an economic threat, but those who successfully pursue a different way of life threaten the British sense of righteousness. One politician, Margaret Thatcher, accurately expressed this fear when talking about racial tension in Britain[3]:

> 'People are really rather afraid that this country might be swamped by people of a different culture. The British character has done so much for democracy, for law, and done so much throughout the world that if there is any fear that it might be swamped, then people are going to be rather hostile to those coming in.
>
> We are a British nation with British characteristics. Every country can take some small minorities, and in many ways they add to the richness and variety of the

> country. But the moment the minority threatens to become a big one, people get frightened.'

This expresses the human need to feel at home in one's country and to believe that one's customs and norms (e.g. 'democracy', 'law') are inalienable. To have this challenged would mean our returning to the condition of wanderers and fugitives on the face of the earth with nothing to shield us from chaos.

The use of race to identify alien cultures has taken on particular importance in the modern world. People have always identified outsiders; the existence of the outsider defines the boundary of one's own society and reinforces one's own sense of cultural identity. But modern international cosmopolitan culture makes it rather difficult to find outsiders for many people have a western-type education, believe in science and technology, wear modern clothes, and in general have a modern appearance and outlook on life. Politicians, businessmen and trade union leaders can communicate easily with their counterparts in virtually every other country of the world, and people begin to wonder what makes their own country unique. Mankind as a whole is a rather too vague, intangible and amorphous thing with which to identify – people want something closer to home. In Britain, national values and characteristics were first exported via the empire to half the world, and now the remaining characteristics seem to be in danger of extermination by incorporation into the European Economic Community. Or so many people feel. As other distinguishing characteristics of Britishness become harder and harder to find, the one thing that seems unchanging is skin colour. People want to preserve their national identity not only from international mass culture, but also from invasion by other, ethnic cultures, and the simplest way to do this is to exclude those of a different colour, thinking that by this method one has identified an outsider.

It is important to realise that this is not an intellectual matter which can be dealt with by reason and education or by facts and figures. The driving force underlying racialism is a fear of insecurity which is fundamental to the human condition. The last thing people want is to understand[4]:

> 'There is no question here of reassuring the people or of demonstrating the reality of a situation to them; nothing could upset them more. The point is to excite them, to arouse their sense of power, their desire to assert themselves, and to arm them psychologically so that they can feel superior to the threat.'

What courses of action do societies take to erase the threat that other cultures pose when they come too close? Let us look now at four of the most common – extermination, assimilation, apartheid, and romanticism – all of which refuse to face up to the root problem. I will describe all of these policies from the point of view of the more powerful culture, for usually the politically weaker group has little option other than to accept the dominant groups' policy or to react against it; they are not usually in a position to inaugurate policies of their own.

1. *Physical extermination*

This is the simplest way of plucking out the thorn from one's cultural flesh. Unfortunately, it is also common, with the Nazi extermination of the Jews and the even more effective and almost complete American extermination of the Red Indian being only two examples that come readily to mind.

Extermination need not be crude and brutal in appearance; it can be disguised as humane. Thus a British National Front policy document 'advocates the repatriation, by the most humane means possible, of those coloured immigrants already here'. A policy of humane extermination of the aborigine was the official policy of Australia in the early decades of this century; popular ideas about social evolution and the survival of the fittest enabled white Australia to believe that the aborigine was an inferior race which, in competition with the white race, was bound to die out sooner or later. A policy of 'protectionism' was embarked on which essentially meant easing the deathbed agonies of the aboriginal races. The earlier expropriation of their land could be justified on the basis that the future of Australia was to be in the hands of the superior race; there was little need to educate the aborigine, nor to integrate him into a society in which he would have no future. So he was shunted off onto reserves of the poorest land and given food and welfare handouts, in the belief that this was the most that a humane and Christian society could do for a race that was soon to die out anyway.[5]

2. *Assimilation: cultural extermination*

Such policies of physical extermination or repatriation are viewed with horror by today's liberals, who believe that members of minority cultures in a white industrial society should become full members of the dominant society. Thus in Britain, it is often argued that compensatory education and other services should be made available to black immigrants so that they can participate fully and on equal terms with whites. This sounds very liberal and enlightened until one realises that it is rarely advocated that native whites be given education and facilities to participate on equal terms with immigrants in *their* culture. The effect is to destroy the immigrants' culture and preserve ours; the threat of the immigrant is as effectively removed as if he had been repatriated.

This is perhaps most clearly seen in the matter of language. What is usually advocated is special tuition for immigrants so that they may learn English; rarely if ever is it suggested that, in high density immigrant areas, local authorities should make all public notices and signs bilingual or that the immigrant tongue should be taught to white children at school. This may sound absurd, but Welshmen who are aware of the English attack in past years on their native tongue will get the point, while the Swiss know that it is quite possible to run a country with four official languages. The English, even in these days of devolution, seem incapable of living with cultural and linguistic diversity. Having succeeded in imposing their language and culture on half the world, they retain a colonial mentality in which the loss of Empire is bad enough but the loss of the monopoly within England of the English language and culture is the very last straw.

The English are among the worst in this respect because as one-time imperial rulers of the world they have most to lose. (Although myself English, I found six years living in Scotland most revealing of the cultural imperialism of the English.) But cultural imperialism is not just an English trait. Let us return to Australia again: the earlier policy of protectionism has now been replaced by assimilation, in which the stated policy of the Federal Government is that

> 'all persons of Aboriginal descent will choose to attain a similar manner and standard of living to that of other Australians and live as members of a single Australian community – enjoying the same rights and privileges, accepting the same responsibilities and influenced by the same hopes and loyalties as other Australians.'[6]

In striking contrast, this hope that aborigines will abandon their manner of living is not expected of European immigrants to Australia, for whom the federal policy officially states:

> 'No migrant is expected to disown his former cultural identity, the heritage of customs and traditions that are the links of the centuries. Indeed these living links with the cultures of the older lands are welcomed in our evolving Australian way of life.'

The cultural identity of the individual is therefore welcomed if he is white and abhorred if he is brown; the intention of the policy is a broadly homogeneous white Australian culture. White Australia's desire to link itself with 'the heritage of customs and traditions that are the links of the centuries' apparently extends only to a few centuries of European history and not to the more than 200 centuries of indigenous human occupation of Australia. To this end, the aboriginal is to be assimilated into the white culture.

3. *Apartheid: separate development*

This section will not dwell long on apartheid, for it is already one of the most discussed issues of our time. Although white liberals in Europe think that apartheid is the opposite to assimilation, and indeed it is the oppposite in method, it shares with assimilation the intention of protecting the dominant culture from the culture of the less powerful group. Assimilation destroys the weaker culture; apartheid simply removes it from sight. Apartheid is abhorrent to liberal assimilationists not because it is so different but because it is so explicitly unashamed about what it is doing. It is not discreet.

Extermination, assimilation and apartheid all fail to tackle the root problem of insecurity that close contact with other cultures engenders. None of these policies attempts to deal with this fundamental insecurity; each simply tries to ensure that different cultures do not get too close, or if they do get close that the weaker culture will have become so emaciated as not to pose a threat to the dominant culture. It can be argued that, given our unwillingness to face this fundamental insecurity, we will have to choose between one of these three policies in one guise or another. If this is your position, then be careful to distinguish two very different breeds of argument. First there are those who argue for a particular policy and at the same time argue for the economic resources to back up the policy. One example would be those who argue for apartheid and native homelands but who also advocate a just sharing of the land such that the weaker group gets as good and as much land as the dominant group and such that the sharing out of the land takes cognisance of the weaker group's traditional concept of property and of land as well as of the dominant group's legal and economic traditions. Another example would be those who argue for assimilation and at the same time argue for compensatory education and other facilities to ensure that past injustices and discriminations are made up for and the weaker group really is given equality of opportunity. This is honest apartheid and honest assimilation, and there is probably little to choose between them.

The second type of argument is the dishonest one. Here the virtues of apartheid are preached, but the blacks are given the worst land; such hypocrisy and self-delusion reigns in South Africa. Similarly the virtues of assimilation can be preached without the corresponding effort to ensure that there really is equality of opportunity – the USA from the end of the Civil War in 1865 up to the present Civil Rights Movement has embodied this kind of hypocritical assimilation. One reason for the acrimony felt between advocates of different racial policies is that we think that our opponents are more dishonest or deluded than we are. The white liberal compares what he sees as his honest assimilationism with the dishonest apartheid practised in South Africa and naturally condemns it; the Afrikaner likewise believes himself to be honest and fair in his espousal of apartheid and naturally condemns what he sees as the hypocrisy of the white liberal.

4. *Romanticism*

Extermination, assimilation and apartheid, if successful, have in common a tendency to be succeeded by romanticism. Once there are only a few Red Indians left after racial extermination, only a few Basque speakers left after cultural assimilation, or once Bantu and Afrikaner culture have been effectively separated, then the threat of these 'minority' cultures has been removed and the nearly extinct culture experiences a last twitch before rigor mortis finally sets in. Once the dominant culture has won the war it can afford to be generous to any remaining cultural refugees. We admire the cave paintings of the stone age aborigine and class them alongside our most modern art. We bend over backwards to find truth, meaning and beauty in primitive cultures. Red Indians are major attractions for white tourists who now have nothing to fear from the redskin; traditional Bantu culture features prominently in South African tourist literature produced for white consumption. That becoming a tourist spectacle is often the most lucrative way of earning a living for these peoples demonstrates the state of economic dependence to which they have been reduced. All this is similar in principle to the way in which the defeat of Jacobinism (during which the English banned the wearing of the tartan) led to the control of Scotland by an English landowning class in the nineteenth century; once the English were secure there it became possible to reintroduce the tartan and generally encourage the revival (and even the invention) of traditional Scottish ways. English landowners were eager to dig up Scottish family connections, in much the same way that it would be a matter of pride for an American today to find he was distantly related to Chief Sitting Bull.

But there is a tendency for not only the dominant society but also the weaker group to romanticise its culture and past history. Separatist and nationalist groups the world over are reviving their old traditions in order to restore what they can of their cultural identity. Politically weak ethnic groups, resentful of the way in which the dominant society has written all the history books in its favour, are discovering and rewriting their own history. Recent examples from America are *Roots* and *Bury My Heart at Wounded Knee*, which make up for the lack of official history from the point of view of the black or red American. Minority cultural groups are beginning to use the laws created by the dominant society to win back some of their rights, as in America where century-old treaties are being used in court to protect hunting and land rights of Indians. But all this is likely to be no more than rearguard action to prop up the self-respect of a defeated people and to salve the conscience of the victorious culture. Even where independence has been won (as in many third world countries) or may perhaps be won (Scotland?) there remains alongside the visible rhetoric of national revival the reality of neo-colonialism in which the newly independent country is as tied as ever to the economies of the super-powers.

Toward a plural society

The policies of extermination, assimilation and apartheid all spring from weakness, from the insecurity felt by a society in the face of alien definitions of reality embodied in other cultures. By contrast, the plural society springs from strength, from a sense of security that is not dependent on any one group's values and norms being sacrosanct. A plural society accepts a diversity of ethnic and cultural groups as equal members and is prepared to pay for the added richness they bring with such inconveniences as having more than one national language. Switzerland has already been mentioned; rather than being a chaotic and muddled country as a result of linguistic diversity, it actually has a reputation for efficiency. As an additional benefit, its commitment to Italian, French and German speaking peoples has been a factor in its remaining neutral in the international political scene, and so it has avoided the appalling destruction that the rest of Europe has suffered through war in this century. America is also often cited as a plural society – in so far as racial pluralism has been achieved this has been because America has defined itself as a society of immigrants. Immigrants from Europe were not seen as a drain on the country's resources but as a source of vitality and strength, of energy and enterprise. In so far as it has not achieved racial pluralism this is because the promised land it offered to the free immigrant was based on the slavery and exploitation of the negro.

One of the most articulate formulations of a plural society is the tradition of the Dutch politician and theologian of the last century, Abraham Kuyper, and his twentieth-century followers such as the philosopher Herman Dooyeweerd and some of the Dutch political parties[7]. They recognise the diversity of culture and of religious and political belief, and advocate a political structure which respects diversity at all levels of society. At the level of government, the Dutch have a system of proportional representation that ensures that every minority can have its say, rather than the first past the post system which allows democracy to degenerate into the majority oppressing minorities (which historically is the problem in Northern Ireland). In education, each cultural, religious or political group may run its own schools and is funded by the state in proportion to the number of pupils. This recognises that education is a matter of values and that different groups within society hold to different values; parents have a right to choose which values should govern the education of their children. This contrasts with most other modern industrial societies in which there is state education, with alternative education possible only for the children of the wealthy. This system is honest in that it backs up its programme with equal economic resources and political power for each of the various subcultures within the one society.

Operating this kind of plural society involves many practical problems, but the principle behind it is right. It believes that the unity of a society should not be based on a consensus of all values and a uniformity of culture. It recognises that a society which insists on this kind of uniformity does so because it is fundamentally weak and insecure. The uniform society is like the Tower of Babel, basing its strength on linguistic uniformity and disintegrating as soon as this is taken away. As a Roman Catholic theologian, Juan Luis Segundo, puts it, the Tower of Babel may be contrasted with the coming of the Holy Spirit and the speaking of many languages at Pentecost:

> 'The first (Babel) seems to embody God's "no" to an attempt to build the city of man on a foundation of undifferentiated unity. The second (the coming of the Holy Spirit) seems to embody his "yes" to the idea of constructing the human community on the foundation of the "different languages" that contribute to humanity all the needs and riches of each and every individual, each and every human grouping, each and every community.'[8]

It will not be easy for Britain to develop into a multiracial plural society in which people not only of different colours but also different cultures are allowed to flourish within the one country. The British sense of identity is deeply bound up with an Empire which believed itself to be God-given and which saw it as its duty to 'civilise' the peoples of Africa and Asia. There is perhaps more hope in the United States, but here too the heritage of generations of white superiority cannot be wiped out overnight. This white supremacy is not central to the

American sense of identity, however, which is much more bound up with the idea of America being the country of enterprise, wealth and newness, and the heroes of history who support this identity are the early immigrants and pioneers. In England, by contrast, the idea of English greatness was based on military and naval superiority over other European colonial powers, together with moral superiority over those colonised. Nelson and Livingstone are heroes. The English sense of national self-respect was based on paternalistically stereotyping other groups as inferior (morally, economically, politically and culturally).

A nation that prided itself on being Christian, England conveniently ignored the treatment by Jesus as equals those whom society treated as outcasts. He ate with prostitutes and other social despicables, and he shocked the people of his time by telling them they were more depraved than Tyre and Sidon (the cities they traditionally saw as the very epitome of immorality). By challenging the conventional stereotypes, Jesus challenged the way personal and national identity is maintained at the expense of outsider groups. This kind of stereotyping is central to both the colonial mentality of the nineteenth century and its offspring, the racialism of the late twentieth century.

Cultural Relativism

Contact between different races and cultures need not involve physical proximity. Through books, films, television and education, the Westerner can become aware of the variety of human cultures throughout the world. Similarly, the peasant in the Third World may never have seen a white man but nevertheless he may own a transistor radio by means of which western culture confronts his traditional ways. This second-hand awareness of cultural differences is easily coped with if the competing culture is presented within a familiar framework; such is usually the case with most travel books and documentaries in which the author, publisher or TV producer neatly packages the foreign culture to suit our taste. It is quite possible to sit in one's suburban lounge watching 'The World Around Us' on the telly or reading the monthly offers from the Travel Book Club without having any of one's basic ideas and securities changed.

But in some circumstances people can find this wealth of information disturbing. One such is the study of the social sciences, and especially anthropology, in which the student becomes vividly aware of other cultures. Whereas once anthropology presented other cultures as 'primitive', thereby affirming our sense of superiority, from around the 1920s onwards it has examined other cultures as viable social systems. They have a rationale and a logic that enable them to work, often more effectively and with less pain to their members than our own modern social systems. This easily induces the feeling in the student that not only may there be other ways of living, but that these may be as valid as our own, if not better.

This can produce a variety of reactions. It can be very threatening as it may dispute the values and customs on which he has staked his sense of identity. This is one reason why social science is often seen by non-social scientists as 'dangerous' – it calls into question far too much for some people's liking. One response born of this fear is to assert that there are universals and that all is not culturally relative. This hankering after universals has often been expressed by Christians who, curiously, seem to find cultural variability a problem. I say curiously, because traditional Christian doctrine claims that man's security is not to be found in this world or in ourselves but in an all-loving, almighty God. The antagonism by Christians to cultural relativism derives from their having baptised as Christian the culture of their own society (ch. 9). Thus to question the English (or American) way of life is to question Christianity. But this idolising of one's own society and this seeking refuge in the security it offers is the very opposite of the transcendent security that true Christianity speaks of. The 'universals' that are produced are usually things like 'family life' and 'the value of the individual', and, far from being universal, are straight out of Anglo-American culture. This response to cultural relativism is in principle no different from the racist response to other cultures; in each case there is an unthinking retreat into the security found in absolutising the values of our own society.

There has been some indication in the last decade or two that, as might be expected, humanist intellectuals are searching for some absolute. From having been the most relativistic of disciplines, anthropology is now searching for universals across human cultures; it is joining forces with ethology (the study of animal social behaviour) to find constants across species in, for example, maternal behaviour, aggression, or altruism; and in linguistics, the structuralist school is searching for elements that lie at the root of all human language. In general, the recent attempts to explain social behaviour in terms of biology (mentioned in the previous chapter) represent a shift away from cultural relativism in search of a biological basis that is constant across the whole of mankind. It seems that academics are not satisfied with the contention of cultural relativism that there is no entity or element that can identify us as human. This seeking after universals has flourished in the last fifteen years or so, a period in which the self-confidence of technology, humanism and the consumer society has been severely shaken and in which there has been a failure of nerve by the middle classes in general and intellectuals in particular. With the rejection of transcendental religion, absolutes are being sought in the human world; once it was thought the so-called rationality of modern man presented such an absolute, but with the erosion of confidence in rationality, people have begun looking to other cultures in search of a human absolute. The story of Cain is re-enacted; mankind, having cut itself off from God, finds all is chaos and shifting sand, and sets off in search of a home. Of course, there may well be universal human structures, but the human need for security (itself a universal) imbues the search for cultural universals with sacred significance. The current search for universals is not the disinterested quest that science might have us believe.

Whatever the extent of cultural universals, the extent of cultural variation is certainly very wide. A healthier response to this variability is to ask: given the variations in culture, why are human societies so keen to convince themselves that *their* customs, norms and values are absolute? Why do they absolutise (or as some sociologists would say, why do they reify or objectify) a way of life which is the product of a particular historical situation, which will not last for ever, and which is different from that of neighbouring societies? Why do societies fly against the evidence and absolutise that which evidently is not absolute? In a word, why are all societies ethnocentric? This question is basic, and if honestly faced brings us to a fundamental aspect of the human condition: the ultimately religious need for cultural security. Facing relativism may be uncomfortable, but it is more honest than running away from it.

Finally, knowledge of other cultures can be very positive in that it provides us with a fund of good ideas as to how our own society may be improved. Clearly we cannot import customs lock, stock and barrel from, say, the Amazon jungle to the modern metropolis, but cultures once thought of as primitive may have much to help us with our peculiarly modern problems. 'Primitive' cultures have often achieved a balance with their physical environment from which we can learn; they recognise the value of the extended family and of the local community; they realise that medicine should re-integrate the sick person into the community rather than, as does western medicine, remove him from it; they often achieve consensus over local political decisions and view the mere 51% approval required by western democracy as immoral, which may have something to teach us as our government becomes more and more remote.

This is not a plea for the romanticising of other cultures, which is usually a result of disrespect for them. It is a plea for an honest appraisal of our own society in the light of what other societies might teach us. No society is perfect, all are directed toward their own particular idols and their own particular securities. There is no merit in running down our own society and claiming that utopia is to be found among, say, the Kalahari Bushmen or the traditional culture of Kashmir; there is no garden of Eden to be found in which man has not fallen. Exalting the noble savage is as misleading and dangerous as exalting the superiority of the fair-haired Aryan or the full-blooded Englishman.

8
The Media as Disinfectant[1]

The previous chapter described how the mere existence of other cultures can threaten the security provided by one's own culture. But not all disturbing information need come from radically different cultures; within modern industrial societies there are events and actions which could shatter the tranquillity and security of the status quo. Poverty, bombings, revolutions, mental illness – all raise questions that threaten the world one takes for granted.

In order to cope with such threats, societies set up filtering systems which ease out anything that may act as an irritant or infect their way of life. If the filtering system cannot keep this information out entirely, it will recast the information in such a way as to render it innocuous. Reinterpreting information is safer than trying to block it out altogether, for it is always possible that some information may by-pass the blocking system. It is safer to make sure that members of the society know how to interpret such information.

But who are these guardians of reality? Two of the most important are the school and the family. The young child continually experiences a welter of new sensations and activities and can interpret them in a large number of ways. Like Alice in Wonderland, first time around everything is rather curious and needs making sense of. A major function of school and family is to ensure that the child makes sense of the world in a way that society approves of. The child learns that competition (or co-operation, depending on the society) is good; he learns how to discredit things of which his society does not approve. The western child, for example, learns that democracy is unquestionably the best political system and that communists and dictators are not to be trusted. But it is not just in such obvious matters as politics that the child is inducted into the ways of his society; he also has to master the minutiae of life – how often one should wash, table manners, the symbolic meaning of different forms of dress and address, and so on.

Sociological studies of this socialisation process have usually looked at school and home. This chapter, however, will look at another means of socialisation, a system that filters information for adults as well as children: the mass media, and in particular radio and TV and their reporting of news. The news is crucial because it collates the enormous number of daily events in the world and reduces them to a form which is digestible by the public. The form in which this daily meal of news is presented is central to the way in which people see the world. The radio and TV, and especially the BBC, are of particular interest because, unlike newspapers, they have no formal political slant and therefore are committed to portraying everything of importance that happens in the world. Unlike a politically committed newspaper or censored television in many countries, the BBC is not supposed to suppress the reporting of particular kinds of events. How then does it present events and actions which are threatening to modern, middle-class, humanist, mixed-economy, industrial society?

Formally, the BBC is committed to 'the elimination of bias' in its news reporting. There is a hornets' nest of debate on this question of television bias, with the BBC asserting that bias-free news is possible, and its critics asserting that it is *not* possible. This book sides with those who think that bias-free news is an impossibility – how can every item of information about what went on in the world today be presented? To reduce it to digestible size and form is not like photographic reduction in which all the information is still there but compressed into 25 minutes. Rather, there has to be some network of priorities which enables the newsmen to filter out the vast majority of information. The newsman has to believe that people are interested in and concerned about some things and not others. The trouble is that any modern industrial society displays conflicts of interest between different social groups, and what people are concerned about varies considerably from one group to another. This poses a dilemma for the news collator, and the simplest way out for him is to assume some basic consensus of interest within the nation, so that the news can be selected accordingly. The idea of bias-free news makes sense only if we adopt this assumption about consensus. It is doubtful that such a consensus exists, but even if it does, there is still a problem in reporting events which fall outside the consensus: for example, how can the media report terrorism, dictatorships, communism, vandalism, black magic? Such things threaten the presumed consensus, so how can they be reported in a 'bias-free' manner? It would mean excluding consensus values and presenting such events as normal and comprehensible, just like any other event. I suggest that our vested interest in maintaining the credibility of our own culture and way of life is such that bias-free reporting of threatening events is simply not possible. Somehow or other, such threats have to be disinfected and made less than credible.

A main theme of this book is how, through society, man creates meaning and order out of a world which has become fundamentally chaotic. But in certain situations the media deliberately create meaning*less*ness and *dis*order. When some group challenges the basis of the dominant culture, then one way of disposing of this group and disinfecting its ideas is to render them senseless, portraying their order as disorder and what they see as meaningful as meaningless. This crucial motive underlies radio and TV reporting of events outside the national consensus. Far from being bias-free it is an attempt to disinfect these events and safeguard the dominant cultural consensus.

The ideology of 'bias-free' reporting is actually part of this process of disinfection. It kids the viewer that the news he receives is the only true version of the events portrayed. For example, the use of the term 'terrorist' is presented as a true description rather than a selective use of one term among many (e.g. 'psychopath', 'guerrilla', 'freedom fighter'), adopted in order to impose a particular view on a highly-charged and ambiguous situation. As propaganda, the notion of bias-free news is perhaps no less dangerous than the censorship and conscious propaganda of totalitarian states where the populace may at least realise that what they are getting is selective propaganda, and that there are alternative definitions of reality even if they are not allowed to be mentioned.

This chapter, then, will look at a range of events which are regularly portrayed in the British media as senseless and meaningless, in particular, radical political action, industrial militancy and 'violence' such as terrorism and mugging. (The inverted commas around 'violence' do not mean that terrorism and mugging are not in fact violent, but that the media identify these things as violence in preference to the many other uses of force which could be defined as violent, particularly that used by the state.)

The problem is that if the terrorist, mugger or industrial saboteur *does* have good reason for his actions then we will have to rethink some of our own personal and societal values. If the men of violence have good reason for their values then maybe the reasons we have for holding our values are poorer than we had supposed, which would be just too painful for most people to contemplate. The media know their audience well and so portray violence as without cause or reason. They prefer not to consider the perpetrators of violence as a group of organised people working purposefully toward a rational end. Instead it is assumed that they are deranged individuals who need either locking up (which protects us physically) or psychiatric help (which protects us from the disturbing task of understanding the political meaning and sources of their violence). Of course, not all violence is rational and purposeful, but because of the immediate benefits in discounting the very possibility of reason and purpose, violence is typically reported in such a way that seems senseless from the start. How is this done? Let's look at terrorism first.

Terrorism

Among the most common news items of the 1970s have been incidents of terrorism. The term 'incident' is most important. What we hear about are portrayed as isolated and unanticipated events, and so we get the impression that what is going on in say, Ulster, is a series of incidents rather than an on-going situation. The 'incidents' are depicted out of context, with almost all the emphasis on the consequences rather than on the possible causes of the incident. We hear in great detail what happened after the incident – we are regaled with TV interviews of doctors who have to treat the victims of a bombing, police officers whose job it is to track down the killers, relatives of the dead and maimed, and politicians who make a pretence of ensuring that such things will be guarded against in future. But because we are told little of what led up to the incident, it appears as an unexpected shock.

One reason for this sort of portrayal on the TV is that there is nothing like real action shots for good telly. A bomb blast, a riot, scenes of destruction after the event – these are visually exciting and tailor-made for the medium of television. By contrast, an analysis of the political or economic context leading up to the incident is much less appealing visually. This slant toward context-less action produces just the right effect for discrediting the meaning of the action; as one critic puts it[2]: 'As this coverage takes the characteristic form of actuality without context, it directly feeds our general sense of a meaningless explosion of meaningless and violent acts.'

But it is not just the technology of television that produces this effect. The selection of people to be interviewed is crucial. The ban on interviewing members of the IRA, for instance, means that the IRA's cause is never presented first-hand (and rarely even second-hand); interviewees, however varied in other respects, all condemn the violence of the IRA, and this reinforces the viewer's feeling of national solidarity, that all good men and true are united, and that it is only a lunatic fringe that is attacking democracy.

Defenders of the media claim that programmes other than the news discuss and analyse the historical context of events. But this does not redress the balance for, whereas the news is presented as fact, discussion programmes are presented as mere opinion. Thus a definition of violence as senseless is written in from the start as *fact*, and any other view can finish only second best as more or less informed *opinion*.

Industrial militancy

Much the same obtains in the reporting of industrial militancy. Unofficial or political strikes are newsworthy not because of their causes but because of their effects. A strike by a couple of dozen men will become news not because of the uniqueness or justness of their grievance but because they halt the whole production of a car factory or because there are direct effects on the public. Indeed, if you are not listening or watching rather carefully, you may miss the actual grievance. As a result, strikes (like terrorism) appear without warning, without cause, and therefore without reason.[3]

This kind of presentation protects the cultural norm of middle-class society which asserts that conflict is not inherent in society in general and in industry in particular, but is a temporary aberration; it also asserts that in an era of progress, people have a right to the uninterrupted supply of the goods and services of civilised living. This middle-class view of the world is confirmed when industry runs smoothly, when dustbins are collected, and when coal and cars are available on demand. It is threatening to believe that striking miners or dustmen have a case and that our discomfort is the result of actions by democratic and loyal people, for this would imply that there are inherent contradictions in our democractic consumer society; much more comforting to believe the strikers are being whipped up by a few Soviet-supported agitators. The possibility that the strikers may be reasonable, sensible, responsible people like you and me is given little credence, with strikers being under-represented in interviews in comparison with management, politicians and media-pundits.

Mugging and vandalism

A third news topic which is depicted as senseless is juvenile crime of the mugging and vandalism variety. Ordinary property offences such as theft and burglary rarely hit the headlines for they do not really shock or puzzle people. The Great Train Robbery or a large bank robbery may be news, but people's response is unlikely to be, 'Why on earth did they do it?' It is obvious why they did it, for such criminals are only acting, albeit illegitimately, in pursuit of one of society's cherished values, the acquisition of wealth. Even a measure of violence in pursuit of this, as in the Great Train Robbery, is understandable. These property offences are unlikely to shock, for the criminals are assumed to hold much the same values as ourselves.

Not so vandalism. Why should anyone want to damage or deface property, except in pursuit of its acquisition? Vandalism attacks not particular items of property but society's very concept of the sanctity of property, which is why it is so disturbing and why vandals are typically dismissed as having no possible good reason for their actions. Increasingly they are labelled as 'disturbed' individuals, but what the media mean by this is that *we* are disturbed by the implications of their actions; we cannot cope with our feelings and so we transfer our disturbance to them[4].

Similarly with mugging. People can understand why grievous bodily harm should be perpetrated for the sake of material gain or even, as in the classic murder whodunnit, for personal reasons. But why maliciously attack a stranger with little chance of financial gain? Such a crime threatens not only the liberty to walk the streets alone, but more importantly it threatens the value of respect for the individual. Mugging is felt to be an attack not only on the body, but also on values.

The media dare not depict such crimes in a way that renders them comprehensible. Property and respect for the individual are central values in our society, and people want to believe that anyone who attacks these values must be less than human – lacking in intelligence, reason, sanity, parental love, or some other essential human ingredient. It is altogether too shocking to consider that they may have a good cause. By designating them as irrational, impulsive, senseless or stupid, it is implied that they are animal-like, beastly, and non-human. The assumption here is humanist for if man is essentially pure and good, then the perpetrators of evil and violence must be sub-human or non-human. The naively optimistic humanist view of humanity is protected by taking all evidence to the contrary and translating it into the work of a few sub-human beings.

This may be contrasted with a Christian view of man as a noble creature, but one who abuses and abases his nobility. It is in our human-ness that we love and in our human-ness that we hate, that we heal and that we destroy. We are purposeful, responsible beings whether we are loving or whether we are hating. This means that evil actions are just as human and comprehensible as good ones, and that it is quite possible to explain the actions of violent men without in any way condoning them.

Suffering and forgiveness

Many of the attempts to provide security described in this book have a kickback. The security found in work creates the tragedy of unemployment and the emptiness of retirement; the security found in the isolated family breeds the problems of the inner city, urban congestion, and loneliness; the security of a national heritage can breed racialism. The security preserved by construing fringe violence as irrational and senseless, while highly functional for society as a whole, can be devastating for those few who actually suffer as a result of terrorism or violent crime. People can begin to bear suffering if there seems to be some reason for it, but as soon as it becomes meaningless they ask in anguish 'Why did it have to be me?' They are apparently willing to suffer for a war they feel is just, but when a war appears pointless their suffering and that of their loved ones becomes incomprehensible and magnified beyond measure. A BBC documentary reported a maimed and bereaved victim of the IRA bombing of a Birmingham pub in 1975 who felt that if it had happened as a result of a car accident or something more 'normal' it would somehow have been all right. His inability to find explanations for what had been done to him multiplied his suffering immeasurably.

This is especially true of actions such as bombings and

mugging in which there is no contact or no prolonged contact between the perpetrator and the victim of the violence, for the victim is then entirely dependent on the media for his understanding of what has happened to him and why. (In contrast, the victims of hijacks and sieges often have considerable contact with their captors and may develop an awareness of their cause to the extent of being able to criticise the press interpretation. On the whole it seems that hijack and siege victims cope with their sufferings comparatively well.)

Not only is the suffering of the victims increased by the media presentation, it is also prolonged. Suffering continues if one cannot forgive; and one cannot forgive someone who is a non-person, sub-human and an animal. The suffering of the maimed and bereaved is exacerbated if the violence has been construed as sub-human and therefore unforgiveable. To forgive someone we must feel that his action, though wrong and harmful, was actually initiated by him. Senseless, meaningless behaviour can be initiated only by either non-humans or by sub-humans who did not have full control over their actions; in neither case can forgiveness enter the picture. Thus, in attempting to help society with the human problem of homelessness, the media end up worsening the problem of suffering.

The Causes of Violence

For the sake of the victims, and for the sake of creating a context in which forgiveness is still an option, violence needs to be understood. Violence is thoroughly human behaviour and therefore no less explicable than more sociable behaviour. In explaining violence, the intention is neither to explain it away nor to justify it; all human behaviour is explicable, but that in no way denies the responsibility of the person for his behaviour. Because human beings are purposeful in their behaviour, they are responsible and their behaviour is comprehensible. The aim in explaining violence is to create a structure in which responsibility, justice and forgiveness may flourish.

How then may 'senseless' violence be understood? What

the media portray as irrational are usually actions taken by people as a last resort. It is precisely when someone has tried the usual reasonable ways of acting and found them to fail that he decides or feels forced to use unusual or 'unreasonable' ways, such as violence. If people have tried all reasonable means and find they are still thwarted, this may possibly be because of limited intelligence or imagination, but it may also be because they are in a position where even the most intelligent and imaginative actions are thwarted.[5]

This powerlessness may derive as much from the structure of society as from any personal inadequacy. An example is the position of a racial minority (or majority as in southern Africa) with few or no legal rights; in this situation you try all reasonable means to gain political, economic, legal and social equality, and find you are constantly obstructed. There are two courses naturally left open. One is to give up, to sink into apathy. The other is to start using what the dominant group sees as unreasonable means; if it will not listen to your voice, then maybe it will listen to your gun. Thus in Zimbabwe after years of illegal government, racial inequality, repression of political opponents and failed negotiations to grant black citizens what are internationally agreed to be their rights, black people took up arms in the struggle for liberty. The same story occurs in many other 'terrorist' situations.

In Ulster, the group discriminated against was not the majority but the Catholic minority. The great problem of democracy is what to do when the majority systematically repress the minority, and when constitutional boundaries are so drawn that the minority can barely have a political voice. This has been the situation in Ulster for most of this century; the minority has found ineffective all democratic means to gain their rights, and now some of them feel their only resort is to use undemocractic means. They are in a classic position of societally structured powerlessness. The reluctance of the British media to present the situation in this light may be because it would highlight this weakness in democracy. Democracy is central to our notion of being civilised people, and we have nothing to replace it with. Over the decades, the anti-catholic discrimination in Ulster rarely hit the headlines. For decades the English public were (and still largely are) ignorant of the way in which Catholics were denied political representation and civic equality. So when the bombs came, they came (so it seemed) out of the blue and without cause. In reality the last resort of a desperate human community, they appeared the first resort of pathological maniacs.

A particular kind of socially structured powerlessness has been termed the 'double bind'[6]. In this situation, a person or a group is faced by contradictory demands but not allowed to comment that they are contradictory. One is immobilised into inaction, yet is required to act. The only action that can possibly emerge in such a situation is irrational; it can literally drive one mad. Unlike the political guerrilla who can provide a coherent rationale for his actions, the person escaping from the double bind may have become so confused that he cannot explain his own actions.

Many young people in our society are in such a bind. We stress to boys the importance of a job if they are to grow up into real men (ch. 2), yet they soon become aware that the economy demands that many people work in alienating conditions or not at all. A large number know this to be their fate, but in the age of the expert, of the economist and the statistician, how can they – mere adolescents – comment on their plight? They feel anger, but cannot express this. Condemned to impersonality, without the identity provided by a steady job, they declare their personality with spray cans on public walls for all to see. If there is no way they can distinguish themselves legitimately, then they distinguish themselves from the mass by some outrageous action (ch. 5).

Since violence and unreasonableness arise out of structural situations of powerlessness, the media's suppression of the meaning of violence rests not just on the public's abhorrence of the violence itself, but also on the fear that the unearthing of the causes of violence may expose inherent contradictions within society. To understand the cause of IRA activity highlights the inability of democracy to cope with the oppression of a minority by the majority. To understand the causes of mugging and vandalism exposes the unemployment and alienating conditions of work that are structurally built into advanced industrial economies. A society needs to be strong to face up to such contradictions, and there is little evidence of such strength in most modern industrial societies.

Ways Forward

How then should we tackle the modern manifestations of violence and unreason?

Firstly, there should be a passion for *justice* that overrides the maintaining of sacred cows (such as democracy). Only when justice is done and seen to be done will there be peace. Unfortunately we seem to rate peace and security before justice.

Secondly, there needs to be *repentance* for past involvement in oppression. This needs to be expressed in positive efforts to ensure that we do not replace the old oppression of one group by the new oppression of another group. Positive steps should be taken now to side with the oppressed and the powerless, and when they in turn have attained their aims, then we move on and support the new powerless. At the end of a war, this may involve changing sides as the one-time oppressors are defeated and become the new oppressed in a blood-bath of revenge.

Ellul[7] points out that there are the known poor and the unknown poor. The Christian presence is to be among the unknown poor, among those whom the world has forgotten. The implications of this for future peace are enormous, for it is precisely the forgotten poor of today who are likely to be tomorrow's men of violence. The famous poor have powerful friends in high places to fight for them, reasonably and peaceably; the forgotten poor have no one.

Thirdly. the poor and the powerless need *a basis for self-respect*. They can fight against their position within society only if they have inner confidence, and this is usually lacking if they have been told by the rest of society for generations that they are worthless. After years of accepting this label of inferiority, their first attempts at self-assertion may be somewhat crude and perceived by others as irrational and violent. The provision of a more worthy self-concept is one of the benefits provided by the various liberation movements, for to identify with fellow women or fellow blacks provides not only the knowledge that one is not fighting alone but it also tells the person that he is worth something.

The sense of worth which comes from the experience of brotherhood (or sisterhood) may also be complemented by the sense of worth which comes from knowing one is accepted by God. One group of exploited workers in Hong Kong found a basis for standing up for themselves in the knowledge that

> 'Men are justified by faith – not by wealth or power or education, but by faith in God's acceptance of them through Jesus Christ even when no-one else appeared to accept them.'[8]

The preaching of the Christian gospel can be a powerful liberating force, for it tells the person that he is worth something, whatever others tell him to the contrary or whatever they do to him. Rather than being used to make him accept his lot (religion as the opium of the people), this knowledge of inalienable worth in the eyes of God can provide the inner confidence that the liberation struggles of today need. Perhaps the greatest need of modern man is to know that he is worth something.

This basis for self-respect and security can liberate oppressors as well as oppressed. To have a home ultimately in heaven rather than in this world means that the oppressors have nothing to lose in a revolution. Their rigid refusal to consider the men of violence as rational, human and having a just cause derives from a vested interest in the maintenance of the status quo in which their security lies. Only when we cease to rely on the familiar world of our own culture will we be able to take seriously what the terrorists and the militants are saying, and what the muggers and vandals are confusedly trying to say.

But meanwhile, those without power do not feel fully

human, and those with it do not want to treat the powerless as human. Something is needed to change this so that the poor can discover their humanity while the powerful, together with the man in the street, can discover the repentance, the forgiveness and the understanding that are so needed, yet so lacking, in the world today.

9
Culture Religion

Human beings are essentially religious, prone to elevating aspects of the social world to the level of the sacred. We impute sacredness to events, ideas and institutions because otherwise we would flounder in a structureless world in the painful condition of homelessness that sociologists call anomie. Although our so-called secular society has apparently rejected official religion in the form of church-going and the church no longer has any privileged status within society, religion is still flourishing in the form of the religion of the family, the religion of work, the religion of the individual, the religion of Nature, and so on. These all perform the traditional functions of religion; they give us something to live for and perhaps to die for, they help us cope with suffering and death, they make life meaningful, they make us feel at home in the world, and they give us a place in the world. From the Judaic-Christian view, these religions are idols which make up for the loss of a place in the universe which befalls man as a result of his rejection of God. Religion, of either the traditional or modern type, covers up loneliness and makes life tolerable. This view of religion is close to Marx's view of it as alienating man from his true self and comforting him by enabling him to hide from his true condition.

The traditional role of religion throughout human history has been to provide a priesthood and a theology to back up the idols of society. Religion is traditionally integrated into society and functions to keep society going, as what Peter Berger and Richard Neuhaus have called 'culture religion'[1]. This has been observed by virtually all social scientists who have studied religion – from Karl Marx on nineteenth century Christianity, through Durkheim and anthropologists studying primitive tribes[2], to modern sociologists looking at religion in America today.

A Call to Transcendence

It does not take a very searching look at the Bible to find that the Judaic-Christian faith intends something very different from culture religion. Here is a God who is transcendent, who is not the product of men's imaginings but who has revealed himself to man and stands in judgement over human activities. Whereas the traditional function of religion is to ease man's path through this weary world, the God of the Old and New Testaments is one who asks awkward questions of man. Whereas the traditional function of religion is to legitimate human institutions, to give the divine okay to them, this god is singularly unhelpful in this respect. Rather than legitimate human institutions, the God of Israel stood in judgement over them. Rather than support the rich and powerful in society, the law of God came down more heavily on them than on any other section of society. This God constantly resisted overtures by men to co-opt him for their own ends.

Nowhere is this more clearly seen than in the institution of kingship, which the God of ancient Israel made very clear was not a divine institution. As David Clines puts it:

> 'Israel was unlike most of her Near Eastern neighbours in recognising that in her case kingship had an historical origin. It was not part of the divinely established order of things, 'lowered from heaven', as the Sumerian phrase had it, or an essential and most immemorial element in the social fabric, as was the case in Egypt. In Israel the kingship was an institution whose origins lay in the relatively recent past, and of which it was well-known that it arose to meet a specific historical necessity: the threat of the Philistines.'[3]

The Old Testament account of the setting up of the Israelite kings is a thoroughly demythologising one. It rejects utterly the notion that the king was divine or semi-divine, specially beloved of God and requiring worship from his subjects (the kind of attributes that were quite normal among Israel's neighbours). Instead, the prophets were constantly criticising, if not the institution of kingship itself, at least many of the Israelite kings. And the law provided in Deuteronomy 17.14-20 gives the king no special rights at all and burdens him with a whole array of responsibilities – 'a conception of the monarchy so low-key as to amount almost to a death by a thousand qualifications'. Rather than being special, the king is to be no more nor less than the model Israelite. Overall, the Scriptures take a rather ambivalent stance toward the institution of kingship; while recognising its legitimacy, they also recognise it to be a human rather than a divine invention and not to be glorified. Kingship may not be a typical social institution, and it is difficult to generalise to other social institutions from it, but the attitude of ancient Israel to kingship does demonstrate the possibility of an approach to social institutions that was quite extraordinary in the ancient world, and still somewhat unusual even in the modern world. We know today that modern institutions are man-made and we do not bring God in to back them up, yet nevertheless we tend to absolutise them and see them as sacred.

The religion of ancient Israel desacralised not only human institutions, but also the natural world. It was common in the ancient world for nature to be seen as divine – astronomical bodies, animals, trees, and so on could all be seen as sacred – and it was for this sacralising of nature that the prophets so consistently attacked the worship of Baal. To the Egyptians, the River Nile and the sun were sacred for it was from the South that the life-giving waters came. By contrast, Israel, while not devaluing the importance of sun and water for sustaining life, saw these as the gifts of a transcendent God rather than as themselves divine. Only God was absolute, sacred and worthy of worship; as was constantly reiterated, the Lord their God was one God, a jealous God who desired the Israelites to have no other gods. Nature and society were important because they had been brought into being and were sustained by this God, but they were not themselves God. The wilderness, for example, was a place where one met God, since the wilderness was where the seeker after God could get away from the competing demands of society, but the wilderness was not itself God. To use the phrase of Max Weber, the world had been disenchanted: the spirits had been driven from the forests, and the altars to human achievement thrown down. This is what the prophets were constantly up against – a sacred world full of competitors for the worship that was solely due to God.

In the biblical view, the world is an ambiguous place. On the one hand it is made by God for us to enjoy, and at every turn it points to the love and majesty of God. The world is the provider of symbols by which man can understand and know God; God is seen as a father, Lord, a rock, a shepherd, the living water, and a whole host of other images, every one of them drawn either from nature or society. Jesus' parables make constant use of the natural and social worlds in order to provide pictures of what God is like. (A modern example of the way in which literally everything in the world can become a pointer to God are the prayers of Michel Quoist which revolve around meditations on such mundane objects as telephones and blackboards, thus showing that not only God's creation but man's also can point to God.[4]) Thus the whole world can be a symbol, important in its own right, but also witnessing to a god who transcends it.

On the other hand, once the world is separate in man's mind from awareness of God, then the world becomes autonomous. The world itself rather than God becomes the focal point, the point of orientation, and consequently itself becomes sacred. By creating a world which was categorically different from God its creator (as opposed to pantheism in which God and the world are one), God took a risk, for he offered man the possibility of accepting the creation and ignoring the creator (an option not open in a pantheistic world).

The world is ambiguous because man is morally ambiguous – on the one hand he can submit his life to

God, in which case the world becomes a symbol of the divine providing windows into the transcendent; on the other hand, man can set himself up in place of God, in which case the world becomes autonomous and sacred. In other words, the biblical God says to man, 'The world is a fine place in which everything is very good and in which there are lots of things to do – only don't make a religion of any of them, because then you will ruin the whole show.'

For the man of faith then, there is a constant tension with the world. As St. Paul said: 'Do not be conformed to this world, but be transformed by the renewal of your mind, that you may prove what is the will of God, what is good and acceptable and perfect' (Romans 12:2). Goodness and acceptability are to be defined by God, not by society. The New Testament depicts a band of believers and a teacher who were not concerned to be successes by the standards of their society. Their faith played down the importance of cultural values such as financial wealth, wisdom, family life, and a secure place in society; none of these things was sacred to them. Although good, they were not essential for the man of faith, and could be done without if that were the will of God. For example, Jesus said that it was hard for a rich man to enter the kingdom of heaven, that love for family could come between a man and God, and that those who were persecuted by society for his sake could rejoice and be glad. Paul added that the early church contained few who were wise according to the standards of the culture of the time, and that the foolishness of God was wiser then men[5].

These are harsh sayings, for it is precisely these things – material security, love for family, a settled place in society and being accepted by one's fellow men – that make life tolerable. To give them up would make life not worth living, and would certainly reduce people to a state of anomie and structurelessness in which there is nothing left to live for and life itself would appear meaningless. Jesus was well aware of this when he called men to give up everything and follow him. He said (as cited above) that it is easier for a camel to go through the eye of a needle than for a rich man to enter the kingdom of God, and he made it equally plain that it was similarly difficult for the happy family, the wise man, or the man who has a settled place in society. At which the disciples were naturally astonished, and asked whether anyone at all could therefore be saved; to which Jesus replied that 'with men this is impossible, but with God all things are possible'.

The extent to which we depend on a settled place in the social structure, and the pain, suffering and meaninglessness that ensue when this is lost, are nowhere better portrayed than in the story of Job. He lost his health, his family, his possessions and everything that made life worth living. His comforters assumed that to have lost all this identified him as morally culpable and so Job found himself a social outcast. Further, he did not know the meaning of his suffering which was thereby magnified. But stripped of all the cultural artifacts that clamoured for priority in his life, Job eventually found God and everything was restored to him twice over. The message is plain: seek first the kingdom of God and get this priority right, and then you will be in a position to enjoy the gifts of God. Only when man has found his true home in God is he free to go out and enjoy the treasures of the house.

Christ calls man to use the things of the world, but without believing in them and without raising them to absolute status. This is psychologically very difficult. For example, it means that the person called to be a politician is not to believe that politics is the most important thing in the world. It means that we are to work, knowing that nothing of ultimate value can be gained because everything of real value has already been given. This involves a constant tension, a running transcendental critique of everyday activities; rather than justify our everyday lives, Christ constantly calls us to question them.

Culture Religion

But human beings do not like tension. They would rather convert the searing critique of Jesus into a religion that accommodates itself to the world, and this descent into conformity with the world is one of the most recurrent temptations to have faced the church. Faith in God thereby becomes a religion which, like all other social institutions, comforts us that all is well with the world. When sociologists claim that the church is functioning in this manner (injecting sacred meaning into human culture), the reaction of Christians should not be denial but serious self-examination. Only then have Christians the right to remind the sociologists that Christianity may possibly not be a religion and that the Bible specifically rejects the culture religion that the sociologists are so fond of unearthing. If the sociologists cannot see this, the fault lies with the church and with Christians for not having manifested the transcendent faith to which their God calls them.

Where then do we find culture religion today? Not in those non-western countries in which the church is actively persecuted since, in such countries, culture rejects Christianity and there is little possibility of alliances between culture and Christianity. The tension with society that Christ demands is reciprocated by society, and overtures for alliances are rare from either side. Perhaps this is why Christ said, 'Blessed are you when men revile you and persecute you'? But in modern western societies, in which Christianity is allowed, we find all sorts of unholy alliances between church and culture, operating at every point of the theological spectrum, from conservative evangelical to liberal to Roman Catholic. Let us look at some of these alliances.

The middle class church

A quote from John Wesley, the early Methodist leader, depicts the unfortunate love affair that the church has had and continues to have with affluence[6]:

> 'Wherever riches have increased, the essence of religion has decreased in the same proportion. Therefore I do not see how it is possible in the nature of things for any revival of religion to continue long. For religion must necessarily produce both industry and frugality, and these cannot but produce riches. But as riches

> increase so will pride, anger, and love of the world in all it branches. How then is it possible that Methodism, that is, a religion of the heart, though it now flourishes as a green bay tree, should continue in this state? For the Methodists in every place grow diligent and frugal; consequently they increase in goods. Hence they proportionately increase in pride, in anger, in the desire of the flesh, the desire of the eyes and the pride of life. So, although the form of religion remains, the spirit is swiftly vanishing away.'

Wesley's answer to this was for the newly-found riches of Christians to be given away, but history attests that rather more was in fact saved or spent, thus confirming Wesley's fears that true faith would wither as Christians became more and more seduced by worldly wealth. Christians have tended to move up the social scale and adopt a new and more middle-class lifestyle.

In the modern context, perhaps the wife is released from some of the daily grind, maybe a car or a second car is bought, one's children's education becomes a priority, and promotion at work comes one's way. As a result of all this, the Christian family is likely to move house to a new area, where their new neighbours are likely to share their standard of living and aspirations – they too have tumbler dryers, second cars and better jobs. And with all this, our Christian family will likely join a new church, more middle-class in membership and attitudes than the one it has left behind. Given the way in which cities are often segregated on class lines (ch. 4), it may be difficult for the family to keep in touch with former friends. Thus there is a steady drain of church members out of the poorer areas, and the church in general becomes more and more middle-class.

This cycle can repeat itself. After a while, suburban middle-class churches may become aware that the gospel is scarcely touching some of the less well-off areas. So they set up missions in slum areas, youth clubs for youngsters in trouble with the law, or they establish new churches in new housing estates or in the decaying areas in the middle of town. These churches may grow and thrive, but no sooner has this begun than indigenous leaders are up and away, for they in their turn are 'bettering themselves' and have joined the trek to the suburbs.

Christians may not be aware of the extent to which they have conformed to a middle-class lifestyle. So many of the public values of society are middle-class that these values, which are far from inevitable or God-given, are taken for granted. Some Christians, because they have one or two taboos such as not drinking or swearing which set them apart from other people, are able to convince themselves that they are not conforming to society. By focusing their attention on such differences as their attitudes to gambling or drink, they ignore the way in which they have unconsciously absorbed their neighbours' views on work, the family, politics, race, class and virtually everything else. They strain out a gnat and swallow a whole cultural mule.

Sects, denominations and churches

Not all Christians, however, end up in the middle-class. But what is noticeable, especially within Protestantism, is that Christians in different socio-economic groups tend to belong not only to different churches but also to different kinds of churches. Those at the bottom of the social scale tend to belong to what sociologists call the sect type – a small exclusive group that sees itself as containing the only true Christians. Its members know where they are going. They know that, though despised by society, they are on their way to heaven; or perhaps they firmly believe the second coming is soon and that the social tables will then be turned. This type of exclusive group provides its members with a strong sense of self-respect and dignity which is denied them by society, and to this end it is crucial that the boundary between the sect and the surrounding culture is very sharp.

Whereas the sect provides for the needs of specific marginal groups in society, the denomination is a bigger and more amorphous affair. It contains within it a greater diversity of doctrinal points of view, and has a more elaborate organisational structure; it will have a printing house, a theological college and so on, all at national level. It will be tolerant of other denominations and not see itself as the only body of true Christians. Its members will be typically solid working-class or lower middle-class.

In some societies, there is a third type – the national church. This is most clearly represented by the Roman Catholic church in countries such as Ireland, but also by the Church of England and the Church of Scotland in their respective home countries. Unlike the denomination, the established church does not see itself as competing with other churches for it believes itself to have a historical right to religious pre-eminence in that country. Whereas the typical sect member was converted to Christianity and the typical denomination member has a parent or grand-parent who was converted, the typical church member was born into the church simply by being a member of society. If you are English and belong to a certain social group, you are automatically baptised and almost as automatically confirmed into the Church of England. The member of the upper middle class or the upper class who presumes his inherited privileged position within society to be right and proper finds it most appropriate that he should also have the right by birth to become a member of the church.

Thus Christianity is divided into several culture religions within the one society. This is sad for two reasons: firstly because the church should not be subservient to culture, and secondly it should not be divided (although of course there should be scope for diversity within it). The two are not unrelated; if there is little unity between different cultural groups within society and if different sections of the church embrace different cultural identities, then this societal conflict will be reflected within the church. As H. Richard Niebuhr puts it[7]:

> 'The organisation which is loudest in its praise of brotherhood and most critical of race and class discriminations in other spheres is the most disunited group of all, nurturing in its own structure that same spirit of division which it condemns in other relations.'

And Francis Schaeffer notes[8] that a world which has

abandoned the possibility of absolute truth is not at all interested in doctrine; but it is also a world greatly troubled by racial, class, international and ideological divisons and is looking for a way in which one person can love another, in which there can be a basic unity between persons even though they may disagree on various matters. It is only if the church offers a prototype of this kind of plural society that the world is likely to take any notice of it. The calling of the church to love and to unity is expressed by Jesus:

> 'I pray . . . for those who believe in me . . . that they may all be one; even as thou, Father, art in me, and I in thee, that they also may be in us, so that the world may believe that thou hast sent me' (John 17.20–21).

> 'A new commandment I give to you, that you love one another; even as I have loved you, that you also love one another. By this all men will know that you are my disciples, if you have love one for another' (John 13.34–35).

But the more the church deteriorates into functioning as a crutch for the cultural identities which divide people (black from white, working-class from middle-class) the less love and unity there will be among and between Christians. This is not a side issue; it is central to the gospel.

The national church

A third level at which the church can be and has been culturally co-opted is that of the nation state. In addition to identifying with social and economic groupings, the church may identify with the political grouping of the nation-state so that patriotism and religion go hand in hand. 'For God and country' is the motto. In contrast to the biblical writers who at different times advocated many different political systems but always declined to ideologise or absolutise any one system, national religion believes that one particular political system is God-given. 'God is on our side', it believes. For example, evangelicalism in the United States was co-opted into the cold war which became a holy war in which to fight against communism was to fight for Christ. Similarly, some white southern African churches have backed the idea that what is being defended there is not white supremacy and greed but 'Christian civilisation'. And much the same was true in nineteenth century Britain when the church happily went along with the ideology that Britain's military and economic superiority in the world was woven of the same cloth as its so-called Christian morality; as the colonies expanded, the Bible travelled the world along with the gun and the railway, but instead of standing in judgement over them it sanctified them.

Although it may be more or less pro- or anti-Christian, society cannot itself be Christian. The heresy of national religion is its belief that its own particular nation is Christian. This belief is typically used to block social change, because by definition any other kind of society or any other ideas about how to run society cannot be Christian and must be wrong. One's own civilisation is believed to be Jerusalem and all others are manifestly Babylon, thus ignoring the biblical portrayal of Israel in which there was always an element of both Jerusalem and Babylon. One's own civilisation is believed to be perfect, and one is blinded to the possibility of constructive criticism. In sum, one's own civilisation is believed to be heaven on earth.

Theology of liberation

If the national church is a culture religion of the right, then the theology of liberation can easily degenerate into a culture religion of the left. The two are essentially the same, for the theologians of liberation also believe there can be heaven on earth, and that one political system is without doubt the best and the only one worth fighting for. The only difference lies in which system is thought to be absolute, but this difference is as nothing compared to the common mindset that absolutises the idea of political heaven on earth. Seen in this light, the otherwise remarkable about-turn of the Roman Catholic church in Latin America in the last decade from being the pillar of neo-colonialism to being full of revolutionary talk is not so surprising. If the church and politics are in league one with another, and the church's present political partner ceases to be credible, then the easiest thing for the church is to look for another political partner. We see the same kind of culture religion in the belief of some African theologians who have rightly rejected the white colonial idea that western civilisation is Christian but who now claim African culture to be the embodiment of the way of Jesus. The communal aspect of tribal life and its mundane recognition of the supernatural may well be nearer than western neo-capitalism to the way of life of the early church, but there is no one culture that is or ever can be the kingdom of God on earth. Jesus stands in judgement over every single human society.

This kind of theology is very similar to that of American fundamentalism or Victorian religion that supported the political status quo, the main difference being that whereas the religious supporters of the status quo are usually blithely unaware of their complicity in politics, the new liberationists are all too aware of what they are doing and have developed a theology to legitimate it. One wonders whether the blatancy of the liberationists or the blindness of the conservatives is the more culpable.

Both national religion and liberation theology legitimate going to war in aid of creating or defending a 'Christian' society. Both develop theologies which enable people to participate in 'just' and 'holy' wars. Both believe God to be on their side and that taking up arms can be a sacred duty. By contrast, this book argues that if it is wrong to inject sacred meaning into the good things of this world, such as the family or work, then it is even worse to sacralise the evil. If the Christian goes to war he should do so reluctantly, seeing it as the lesser of two evils, and in doing so he should look to God not for justification but for forgiveness[9]. This is bordering on the psychologically impossible, for men generally need justifications if they are to go out intending to slaughter wholesale other men. To win a war with a bad conscience is perhaps unknown in human history; it was, for example, when America ran out of justifications for continuing the Vietnam War that it found it lacked the inner motivation to carry on with it. Perhaps the words of Jesus are again appropriate here: 'With men this is impossible, but with God all things are possible.' If this psychology of war sounds impossible, the psychology of peace that would follow it sounds a good deal more hopeful. During war one would not have learnt to hate the enemy, and, not believing their cause to be holy, the victors would not have an entail of hatred and self-righteousness with which to start the peace. Reconciliation would therefore become a real possibility, and the prostrate enemy would not be kicked in the teeth, thus storing up resentment and bitterness for the future.

The search for relevance

The church feels itself more and more out of touch with modern man, and doubtless modern man feels the same, although he is not bothered about it. Consequently the church attempts to become more 'relevant'. Now if this means trying to address the problems of modern people in the language of modern people, then it is no more than what the church has always been called to. But often it means something rather different; often it implies taking modern modes of thought, especially the scientific and rational modes, as the starting point from which to interpret Christianity. Thus the Bible, church practice and dogma are all filtered through the sieve of rationality, efficiency and science, and anything which can be shown to be unscientific or irrational is cast aside; this is what commonly passes for 'demythologising'. This follows philosophers, such as A. J. Ayer, in the assertion that anything that is not empirically verifiable is literally nonsense[10].

This view that the thought forms of the modern world are the only valid ones is incredibly presumptuous and arrogant, not to mention ethnocentric (the very sins that so-called tolerant, liberal, relativistic modern man accuses the traditionalists of). Attempting to be radical, these searchers after relevance bow down to the sacred cows of modern society and thereby end up being as conventional as is possible. A classic example is Harvey Cox's book,

The Secular City, in which he declares that the characteristic anonymity, mobility and pragmatism of modern urban life are the very stuff of biblical Christianity; but in his attempt to be relevant, Cox has jumped off the biblical reference point of a transcendent God who stands in judgement on the world, including the modern world, and has ended up accepting the plight of modern man not only as a necessity but as something to be welcomed. Cox thus in effect advocates a traditional culture religion which accepts society as it is and provides a theological legitimation for it. Cox perfectly fulfils Marx's view of religion as an opiate that enables man to carry on through a miserable historical situation by conning him that his situation is in fact the benign will of God. Cox is therefore both politically and theologically one of the most traditional thinkers on the market[11].

In the 1950s and 60s when science and technology seemed without question to be the heralds of a new age of prosperity and peace, and when the logical positivism represented by A. J. Ayer provided the philosophical backing for this hope, the approach of Cox and others like him had a certain seductive plausibility, for it bowed to the idols of the day (who, like most idols, were not then recognised as such). Disillusion with science and technology has now set in, however, at least in the intellectual circles among which 'the theologians of relevance' were read; after several decades of technological wizardry, all the future seems to hold is the possibility of nuclear holocaust, ecological catastrophe or starvation for half the world. Technology now has its critics and, especially following the publication of Thomas Kuhn's *The Structure of Scientific Revolutions*, few philosophers believe science to be a continuous and ever upward march of increasing knowledge and control over the natural world. The college-educated young are increasingly turning to mysticism, pre-historic life forces and other esoteric sources in the search for knowledge; they have ceased to believe that science has all the answers. Thus the 'relevant' theologians of the 1960s, interpreting Christianity according to the dogmas of science (or what they thought was science), now appear irrelevant. In a fast changing world there is a word of warning here for anyone who is into culture religion – today's culture may be out of fashion tomorrow, and what is 'relevant' today will be out of date tomorrow; the chances are that it will even be out of date today. History makes culture religionists look a little silly.

Social action

Many of the middle-class culture Christians described earlier have recently woken up to their cultural collusion; especially they have recognised the implications of the private nature of their faith which concentrated solely on personal salvation and personal morality. Among evangelicals, in particular, the 1970s have seen social involvement tacked onto evangelism as the witness of the church in the world. All this may be admirable, but there is a distinct likelihood that they will simply swap one set of societal idols for another. The danger is that in their eagerness to be socially involved and to help solve social problems, they unthinkingly adopt the definition of what constitutes a social problem from the political and media pundits of the day. This climbing on the latest social policy bandwagon has been aptly termed 'me-too-ism' by David Moberg[12]. Thus Christians get concerned about unemployment or the housing problem and engage either in social work providing first aid for those without homes or jobs, or in political action trying to secure more homes and jobs. But this is a kind of co-option by paternalistic welfare statism, or by some other political philosophy. Surely it must be asked why Christians so easily identify with the unemployed or the homeless? Do Christians too bow to the idols of home and work? Surely the Christian contribution is rather to ask why it is that the homeless and unemployed in our society are so crippled? Why does society so elevate a good home and a paid job that those who are denied them are rendered second class citizens? Why is it that people find security in these things? Without doubt, Christians should be concerned with providing jobs or houses, but this may not be what they are called to do as *Christians* but simply their duty as *citizens*. The distinctive Christian contribution may be to ask these rather more fundamental questions that point ultimately to the homelessness of man, to his need for worship and to the Christian gospel that can meet this need. Ultimately, the Christian gospel says that what man needs is not homes or jobs, but God.

Another wing of the social action movement of the 1970s is that typified by the Festival of Light, in which pressure groups strive to maintain 'Christian standards' in the law pertaining to such matters as pornography, abortion and euthanasia. The danger here is the presence of overtones of a national religion, affirming that western society of two or three decades ago was Christian and urging that we should try to rescue what we can of this previous age. Certainly if mass support is to be gained, the so-called 'Christian standards' have to be translated into some set of cultural norms which the presumed silent majority of nominal Christians can embrace. Quite what 'Christian standards' are is unclear, but certainly they would be pretty unpopular. To gain popular support the Festival of Light and its friends are compelled to translate the transcendent demands of Christianity into a culture religion, not because of any inadequacy in the Festival of Light but because of the inherent tension between Christ and the world.

This tension is perhaps most clearly seen in numerous calls in the 1970s for the upholding of the family and of family life. The problem here is that to talk meaningfully about 'the family' you have to talk about the dominant type of family in your own country. There is no such thing as an abstract family, and certainly the Bible does not talk about an abstract family but about the particular families that existed in ancient Israel (ch. 3). The family is already sacred in our society, and the very last thing it needs is further upholding. There is indeed a lot wrong with the family, and its healthy future will be ensured not by upholding it but by placing it under judgement and by providing a critique of it. When an institution is idolised, things inevitably begin to go wrong because too much is expected of it, while other aspects of life are neglected. What such an institution needs is not upholding but a transcendent critique. It may be that as an idol fails to fulfil its promises people abandon it wholesale and swing to some opposite alternative, in which case it would need upholding, but that stage is a long way off with the family. If it is in human nature to sacralise social institutions, then the church must tread very carefully when discussing them. When politicians call the family 'sacred'[13] and in so doing express the feeling of the nation, Christian calls to uphold the family can only be taken to mean that Christians too believe the modern private family to be sacred. This is pure culture religion; Christianity, by contrast, believes only God to be sacred and worthy of worship. This is central to the Christian message, and only when this is understood can the family and other social institutions find their rightful place – considerably lower than the angels.

10
Conflict and Change

So far, this book has discussed some ways in which the sacred in modern society provides a stable and orderly home that keeps chaos and anomie at bay. This is indeed what mankind wants the sacred to provide. But there are also other, unintended, consequences of the sacred, not the least of which are exploitation, social conflict and social change.

The way in which the sacred produces stability and order, rather than conflict and change has been focused on for two reasons. Firstly, it is hoped that by understanding the place of the sacred in society the reader will be helped to understand the world he inhabits. Assuming that most readers are members of the middle classes of modern industrial societies, and given that such people inhabit stable and orderly worlds, it seems sensible to focus on those aspects of society (stability and order) with which the reader is most familiar.

Secondly, it seems to the writer that there is at present a greater need for a Christian critique of social order than a critique of social conflict. This is because most Christians are at present more critical of social conflict than of social order. They disapprove of industrial strikes, naked class or racial conflict, political unrest and rapid social change; but social order (in the form of family life, the state, work and the church) they assume to be the will of God. Those Christians who *are* critical of the present social order very often borrow their critical armoury lock-stock-and-barrel from not particularly Christian ideas currently fashionable in the bourgeois intelligentsia[1]. One searches in vain today for the basis of a distinctively Christian critique of the social order, which is what this book has tried to begin to provide.

So, this book is about the way in which social order and stability are provided by the idols of the age. To deal adequately with conflict and change would require another book, but it is worth suggesting briefly a few ways in which conflict, exploitation and change could be understood within the framework of this book.

The key is *dependence*. Because the sacred provides the home that mankind seems to need so much, mankind has become dependent on the sacred. The need to bow to idols has placed us in bondage to them; we strive for a life of independence and freedom, but are shackled to a life of need and dependence. Some of the needs that the search for home has engendered have been major themes in our discussion: the need for goods and a physical environment that supports our home world, the need for status in the eyes of others, the need for immortality, and the need to protect our culture from other cultures.

Conflict

An individual or group can meet these and other needs only at the expense of other individuals or groups; the attempt to meet these needs almost inevitably brings people into conflict. Let's look at each of these needs in turn.

1. *The need for goods*

Furnishing the nest, providing the right scenery for the play of life, is crucial if the social world is to remain credible. On the grand scale, this may involve the eighteenth-century aristocrat in landscaping the view from his stately home so that he need not be disturbed by the sight of the lower classes or rival landowners; or prosperous Victorian towns in erecting magnificent municipal buildings to the glory of free enterprise; or nearer home, it may involve the modern private family in surrounding itself with an array of household gadgetry and mod-cons which symbolise the family nest as a self-sufficient and self-contained world. This desire to structure our private and public environments has led to dependence on material goods. In a finite world, this results not only in the depletion of natural resources (as predicted by ecologists) but also in competition over goods in short supply (as studied by traditional economists). This competition involves a conflict of interests and, if we are to believe Marx, economic conflicts are at the root of social conflicts, placing one social class in antagonism over against another. Even if one does not go the whole Marxian hog, it is clear that in a world that believes in the pre-eminence of economics, the repercussions of economic conflict are not confined to economics.

The problem is that the more goods I have, the less you have. Of course some deny this, saying that if the size of the total cake is increased then everyone can have more, but looking at the history of civilisation as a whole it is hard not to conclude that the wealth of some is built on the labour of others. Today this is markedly so between rich and poor nations.

By itself, private charity is no solution to this. Too often, after putting their money into the collecting tin, donors have a warm feeling that they have been charitable, whereas a more appropriate but less comforting response would be communal and political repentance for the international economic order. At Christmas, Oxfam posters remind us that while we are eating our Christmas dinner, children in other parts of the world are starving; but instead of the causal links between these two facts being understood, donors see themselves as participating in the Christmas spirit of generosity. One wonders whether the name of the Christian charity Tear (The Evangelical Alliance Relief) Fund is thought to symbolise tears of personal pity or tears of communal repentance? In all this, are we repeating the mistake of our Victorian forebears in their response to the class inequalities of their age? Whereas what was needed was repentance (a turning around in action as well as feeling) for their part in exploitation, what they offered was typically a little self-congratulatory philanthropy. Plainly there is a need for philanthropy, for binding up the sores of the sick and providing relief for the starving, but without a radical turning from building our wealth on their poverty one can only question the motives of philanthropy.

2. *The need for status*

If some would question the assertion that I can only be rich to the extent that you are poor, surely things are clearer when we move from the need for goods to the need for status. Status really can be a zero sum game: my status depends on your deference to me, so what I gain in status you lose. Your deferring to me may provide you, as it does me, with a settled and stable place in the social hierarchy (the serf as well as the squire knew where he stood), but your place may not be a very enviable one whereas mine may be highly prestigious. The search for status involves my becoming superior, which involves your becoming inferior. Chapter 5 discussed the desire in individualist societies for personal distinction, the desire to distinguish oneself, but in order for one to be distinguished there must be an undistinguished mass from which one stands out. Status may provide me with a good place in the world, but only at the cost of providing you with a less good place.

The same is true of immortality and fame. Modern society offers no structured way in which everyone can be remembered by posterity, and so to the degree to which one person is remembered then others are forgotten. This too can be a basis for social or interpersonal conflict.

3. *The need to protect cultures*

It was mentioned earlier that all societies are ethnocentric, believe their values to be right, and resist invasion by other cultures. Many of these invasions come from other societies, but urban industrial societies are large and complex, containing within them a variety of different cultures and subcultures. The dominant group within such a society therefore needs to protect its culture from infection by other cultures and subcultures. In Europe and America, the dominant culture is white, male and middle-class, in that these groups control the institutions that define reality for the population: institutions such as education, government, advertising and the mass media. (The main exception to the power of this group to define reality lies within the family, where women are crucial to defining reality for children and where different class and ethnic traditions may be handed on.) In order to maintain the dominance of white, male, middle-class culture, members of other groups are manipulated into behaving according to the norms of the dominant group. Women are expected to behave like men at work, black children are taught to become like whites at school, and working-class people are seduced into adopting middle-class aspirations through education and advertising.

This too can be self-defeating. The more the dominant culture strengthens itself by undermining alternative cultures and extending its tentacles into ever new areas of life, the greater the loss of vibrancy in the other cultures within society. Once the weaker groups have realised what is happening, that their own cultures are being undermined, then they may start opposing this trend and overt conflict may ensue. Thus may be born ethnic independence movements, liberation movements for minority groups, and some working-class political movements.

Now conflict may ensue as a result of the attempts of different groups and individuals to fight for and protect their own particular social order. Man has chosen to build his social world with resources (not only material resources but also resources such as status) which are finite and in short supply; often with negative results.

A just society will frankly recognise material and cultural conflict, and will institutionalise means to regulate it in a fair manner. But it is hindered in this by the sacred, for the sacred hides the existence of conflict. The sacred provides an altar or altars at which the whole population worships and thereby induces a false feeling of unity within society. But it does not thereby eradicate conflicting interests. The sacred induces a false consciousness (in the Marxist sense) about the identity of interests among all groups within society and hides the exploitation of one group by another. The sacred is therefore very much to the benefit of ruling and exploiting groups, and is largely maintained by them. (This analysis draws heavily on that of the New Left in that cultural hegemony is perceived to be a fact, an undesirable fact[2]. But there is a difference in that the New Left underestimates the extent of the resistance to the undermining of society's ideological superstructure (the sacred) which is maintained by the ruling classes, for the masses too are as dependent on the sacred for their sense of home as the ruling classes are for their material gain.)

Personal conflict: from sociology to social work

Not only does the sacred both foster and at the same time hide social conflict, it can also induce personal conflicts. Life may seem fine for the majority who gladly worship at the sacred shrines of society, but what of those who of their own free will decline to worship: people as disparate as the youthful vandals of the western world, who refuse (at certain times and places at any rate) to worship the god of property, or the Soviet dissidents who refuse to worship at the shrine of the state? What of those who, out of no desire of their own, are refused access to the shrines: the unemployed or minority groups who are denied work, for example? How do such people experience their situation?

The experience of becoming either voluntarily or involuntarily a social deviant and outcast often involves emotional depression and personal disintegration. Without the presence of the sacred to integrate life, things begin to fall apart. Anyone who has lost that round which they had previously focused their life (whether job, spouse, child, reason or religion) finds life to be potentially or actually without meaning. In addition, he or she feels no longer able to cope with life, for what had been an essential resource has now been denied.

A lot of depression may be traced to this. Society has a vested interest in seeing depression as a pathological state from which the sufferer must be rescued as soon as possible (for example with drugs) so that he may be quickly re-integrated as a normal worshipper of the idols of the age (especially the idol of happiness). But a more constructive approach would be to see the depression as a potential turning point in a person's life. It provides him with a golden opportunity to review his life and ask whether he really wanted to focus so much of life around that which is now lost. Your child has died – but why did you invest so much in it? You failed your exams – but why did you so want to achieve? Your future seems in ruins – but why did you trust your reason to plan and predict the future? You have become unemployed – but why was so much of your self-respect bound up in a job (a job which may well have involved exploiting others or producing tools of destruction such as cigarettes or armaments)? Your house burns down – but why had you invested so much emotionally as well as financially in your house and its stage-props?

It is in the nature of idolatry that people take their idols for granted. Their social milieux are filled with fellow worshippers and their common idols seem natural and normal. It is only when people willingly or forcibly cease to worship that their priorities are revealed in depth, and it may be only then that they have a real chance to assess their priorities.

This insight has important implications for personal counselling, psychotherapy and social work. These professions could be of great help in enabling the client to 'spot the idol' in his or her life. But contemporary social work and psychotherapy are ill-equipped to do this since they themselves idolise the family and the child. They therefore assume deficiencies in family life and childhood to be the chief contemporary sins, and are professionally and organisationally geared to reducing all personal difficulties to family and childhood problems[3]. This diagnostic and therapeutic procedure derives historically from Freud, but this origin does not account for its present popularity which derives from acceptance of the modern notion of the sacred family and the sacred child. This blinkers these professions from carrying out the much more open diagnostic procedure of 'idol spotting'.

Exploitation

In the present age, people's needs can often be met only by grabbing from others. But it is not only others who suffer; those whose needs are met or are about to be met are also in a precarious position. They need the security and sense of place provided by goods, status and culture, not to mention by idols such as the family and work, and therefore are dependent on these things. And as Mao so correctly understood, those who are dependent get exploited.

Consider some examples. The psychological as well as the economic dependence on paid employment that the idolatry of work induces means that people will accept servile and demeaning jobs in which they are exploited because they would rather have a bad job than no job. The worker's fear of being unable to cope psychologically with unemployment is a card in the employer's pack when it comes to industrial bargaining. The worker's position is weak because he needs work if his life is to remain an integrated whole.

Or take the family. The belief that fulfilment is to be found only within a loving relationship with a sexual partner and in parenthood is continually exploited by advertisers. Almost any product or service can be sold if it is presented as enhancing your love life, your family life or your children's happiness – cars, perfumes, toys, food, life insurance, building society saving accounts, washing machines and so on, ad nauseam. It is precisely because society believes the family to be the place where life is to be lived that adverts can portray so many apparently unrelated goods and services all in a setting of romantic love, happy families and smiling children. Our emotional investment in sexual love, family life and the happiness of children makes us peculiarly vulnerable to the predations of advertisers. Most of the profligate consumption of modern society is not caused by selfishness but by people genuinely believing they are consuming for the sake of their family, their children or their spouse; dare you refuse to buy something if not buying it may prejudice the happiness and health of your child?

Similarly, we experience a need to live in a society whose culture and values are not fraying at the edges. This need is regularly exploited by politicians who claim their policies are the only ones that will keep the country together, are in the national interest or will ensure the protection of dominant social values from immigrants, vandals or terrorists. We have a vested interest in believing our country to be one in which everyone believes in the same values, and we listen to politicians who claim to support such a society. Politicians always support the sacred.

Or we can be exploited by the security that formal religion offers. We so much want to be reassured that our particular values (work, the family, the individual and so on) are in fact worthy that we welcome any religion which provides them with supernatural sanction. People give money, time and effort to this kind of culture religion (ch. 9). This sort of religion is no different from the advertising that prostitutes itself to the idols of the age.

Dependence on the things of this world leads to exploitation because such things are precarious and we fear their being taken away; we fear being thrown out of work, our children not getting the best start in life, or our marriage breaking up. Pretending to provide security against anxiety, idols such as work and marriage become themselves the object of anxiety.

How then can we find a position where we are not open to being exploited? For some the answer is independence. The wife, shocked to find how dependent she has become on husband and family, seeks independence in work; but thereby her new identity simply becomes dependent on her job. Or the man tied to his employers and exploited by them decides to become independent and sets up in business himself; but thereby he simply transfers his dependence from his former employer to his own health, reason and initiative (none of which are guaranteed against the diseases common to late male middle age). And political independence in the former colonies has all too clearly shown that former political dependence on colonial powers has been replaced by dependence on indigenous political élites, while economic dependence on the industrial world (east or west) continues.

Independence is impossible for human beings, for it is always dependence on some new master. Freedom exists only so long as people are dependent on something that cannot be taken away; which is why Christianity claims that trusting an all-loving God whose promises do not fail provides true freedom. As the philosopher Kierkegaard put it:

> To be dependent on his own wealth [*and we may add: to be dependent on work, family, reason, etc*], that is dependence and heavy bondage; to be dependent on God, absolutely dependent, that is independence.[4]

All Change

The inevitable association between the sacred and conflict and exploitation prompts the question whether the sacred may be less stable than it appears at first sight. In fact, change is inherent in idolatry. An idol is created when something which in its right place is a good thing, is overloaded with meaning. The family and the city are classic examples. It is too much to expect such mortal and created things to provide salvation: the idol cannot possibly live up to this religious expectation and so, sooner or later, disillusion sets in.

For example, it is because of an overconfident belief in the power of technology to usher in a new dawn of prosperity for all that recent years have seen stinging attacks on 'the technological fix'. Those whom one would suppose to benefit most from a technological future (the affluent young of the industrial world) turned in the 1960s to nature, to mysticism and to religion. As disillusion arrives, so a new idol (e.g. Nature) is set up which is believed to be the opposite of the discredited idol and therefore guaranteed to provide the salvation that the old one failed to deliver.

It is not just the failure to meet overambitious expectations that leads to social change, but also the tendency of an idol to be glorified and be given excessive power. Eventually this abuse of power provokes a reaction and the idol may be overthrown and, again, what is believed to be its opposite set up in its place.

For example, the glorification of the individual in the last century led to the excessive power of capitalists who then had to be restrained by the state. In its turn the excessive powers taken by the state, particularly in totalitarian countries, have provoked dissidents into proclaiming the value of the individual (ch.5). Or take the city. The power of the city to suck into itself a disproportionate amount of the wealth and resources of a nation, especially of third-world nations, has led the third world to reaffirm the importance of agriculture and of the countryside. Whereas once technology and education, epitomised by the city, were hailed as the saviour of the third world, now many believe the future to lie in agriculture and in the skills and labour of the rural peasant. 'Big is best' is replaced by 'small is beautiful'.

Thus the sacred comes in pairs, each component of a pair constantly firing salvoes at the other, and with dominance oscillating between them from one decade to another. The sacred always exists in conjunction with the profane. Some examples already referred to are the individual versus the state, the city versus the country, work versus leisure, the technological fix versus co-operation with nature, and order versus freedom.

In each case, replacing one by its presumed opposite betrays misdiagnosis of the problem. It is assumed that if, for example, cities are not working properly then cities are evil, or if the family puts too much strain on individual members then the family is evil and should be abolished. This is misdiagnosis because it fails to see that the problem is not the city or the family but the absolute faith formerly put in them, their elevation to the sacred. As a result of this misunderstanding, absolute faith is placed in the alternative which in turn becomes sacred and liable in time to the very same problems of overloading, excessive power and consequent disillusion and reaction.

This means that history often goes in cycles (although a repeat cycle is never a replica of the original). This view is rather different from the dominant modern model of history as a linear evolution toward contemporary civilisation, in which freedom evolves out of oppression, reason and science out of ignorance and superstition, and democracy out of the dark ages of feudal bickering. In this dominant view, freedom, reason and science are sacred, and history is interpreted in terms of these sacreds. The view of history implied in this book, however, refuses to see anything as sacred and therefore refuses to judge history in terms of today's idols.

What kind of time scale is involved in this cyclical model of history? How stable are the contemporary idols described? Two rough answers can be given.

One is that for the time being contemporary idols are massive and virtually immovable. This, for example, is the view of Ellul who sees the idols of technique and efficiency, reason, happiness, progress and faith in Man as pervasive throughout the whole modern world including both east and west, middle and working classes, straight society and the counter culture. He claims that we are so thoroughly socialised into this humanistic and technological consciousness that it is imported even into the protestations of those who see themselves as rebels (as has been argued above in the case of radical ecology: ch.6). Of course, any one of these idols may be expressed in numerous ways; the ideal of happiness, for example, has been expressed in such diverse forms as Jeremy Bentham's philosophy of the greatest happiness of the greatest number, the present-day goals of individual fulfilment and personal development, and the preoccupation today with mental hygiene. In each formulation the cardinal sin is to be unhappy; for this is an offence against the god of happiness.

The other answer, suggested in part by Berger, is that an all-encompassing social universe with supreme idols compelling allegiance existed only in traditional societies. Today by contrast, we have developed the ideal of the individual who alone is able to choose the meaning he gives to his actions. How and where to direct my life is my own choice and cannot, or should not, be dictated to me by society. Indeed not only is the meaning to be chosen *by* the individual self, it can only be truly found *within* the self. In sum, there has been a shift from meaning being *given* by traditional society, to meaning being *chosen* by the modern individual. People worship just as much as ever, but there is now a choice of altars; rather than being required by society to worship a particular god, they are now required to choose their own gods. The shift in Christianity from a Christendom compelling allegiance, to our present system in which the individual chooses his own 'religious preference', is a classic example of the more general shift from given-ness to choice in worship.

This historically unprecedented freedom for the individual to choose where to direct his life is something that many are not prepared for. They grope uncertainly for values and meaning. They wish the social world were more stable and that there were more consensus within society. They find the lack of integration within the social structure disturbing; they experience society as anomic, disintegrating and losing its moral standards. Reality seems fragile.

At first sight these two answers appear contradictory, for the one says that we have no option but to bow to the idols of the age, while the other says that the individual must choose where to direct his life. But they are not necessarily contradictory, for three reasons.

Firstly, the shift from traditional to modern society and from given-ness to choice must be understood as a shift from one ideal type to another. The ideal type is an abstraction and no actual society is either wholly traditional or wholly modern; all societies are somewhere on a line between the traditional and modern types. Present-day industrial societies, while considerably more modern than any other societies hitherto, nevertheless retain many traditional elements. Thus in modern society, meaning is given as well as chosen. Paradoxically for those who believe in individual choice, the value of the individual is itself a given in western society which is not open to question.

Secondly, the picture of individuals freely choosing their own meanings does not mean they are able to choose from an infinite stock of meaning – rather, they must choose from the limited stock provided by society. For example, an individual is not free to believe that the world is flat, or that his children should not be educated, and if he acts on such beliefs the full weight of the law or of social disapproval will fall upon him. The ordinary individual may feel free, but he will discover limits to that freedom as soon as he attempts to worship at altars other than those offered by society.

Thus the task of sociology is to describe the range of idols on offer by society and show how they are differentially available to different groups within society; the task of social-psychology is to describe how individuals choose and create meaning for themselves out of this cultural repertoire. This book has sketched a few of the more dominant idols and a few aspects of the cultural home that modern society offers.

A third way in which the two answers complement rather than contradict each other is that they are describing different levels. At a very basic level, the orientation of society is deeply entrenched in that the belief in Man, the exaltation of Reason and the primacy of the empirical world seem virtually impossible to get away from. They are dey embedded in modern consciousness and so broadly backed up by the social world that they are present even among those who protest against them. Ecologists purporting to believe in Nature actually believe in Man; young people who are 'into' spontaneity or mysticism describe these experiences in a typically modern and rational frame of discourse; and Christians, while officially believing in supernatural doctrines like the resurrection and the second coming, in practice find these to be of little salience in their everyday lives.

But at the surface it may be possible to choose one's idols. Although at a deep level we all believe in Man, at the surface we may have a choice between Man As Individual and Man As Socialist Collectivity. Or, we may all believe in individual fulfilment but may differ as to whether this is best achieved by supporting the family or by abolishing it. There are many different levels of meaning and belief; in general there is most consensus over the deeper, taken-for-granted levels and there is most choice and debate over the surface levels. Since there is most debate at the surface, we get the impression of much dissension within the modern world, while we are blind to what all modern societies share in common. One often observes what Martin Luther so aptly described: people pulling like foxes in opposite directions without realising they are tied together by their tails.

So far, all the chapters in this book have been devoted to describing, within a Christian-sociological framework, how society *is*. This kind of knowledge is essential if mankind is to fulfil the modern dream of taking control of its own destiny and being the architect rather than the victim of social change. We cannot get to where we want to go without knowledge of where we are now.

But the future also depends on our *response* to the present. How one responds depends on one's ultimate commitments, and the final chapter will outline in a little more detail some of the commitments that have guided this book.

11
A Tale of Homelessness: Theological Themes

Running through the book has been the theme that society sets up sacreds through which human beings attempt to come to terms with the problems of homelessness, death and their relation to nature. It was mentioned in chapter one that the sociological understanding of society is enhanced by placing it within a broader, Christian understanding of the human condition, a view explored in this final chapter.

The human condition contains many paradoxes. Human beings are something of a puzzle to themselves and perhaps always have been. There is the puzzle already alluded to of mankind being part of, yet apart from, nature. There is also the paradox that we are capable of so much creativity, altruism, intelligence, etc; yet time and again we stoop so low. The paradox heightens as we note that it is often the most creative or the most intelligent who stoop the lowest. Even more curiously, those who are most loving in one area of life may be most unscrupulous in other areas – the most doting husband and father may also be a crooked politician, a ruthless businessman or a heartless revolutionary.

Such paradoxes, expressed differently at different times, lie at the heart of human experience. Attempting to comprehend and come to terms with them has occupied human beings throughout recorded history, and we have done this, not for the pleasure of abstract philosophising, but so that we may know who and where we are and have the confidence to go out and live. These attempts at comprehension have often been expressed in the form of stories.

Such stories, as told in traditional tribal societies and in ancient Greece and the Near East, have been called *myths* by anthropologists and historians, suggesting not that the stories are untrue but that truth for the hearer lies beyond the literal meaning. Such stories are not told for their own sake, but in order to tell a deeper truth about the human condition. It is sad that today we so often use the word 'myth' in a derogatory sense; this indicates that we believe only the 'facts' that science reveals – we think that because myths are not necessarily factual or scientific, and not empirically verifiable they are therefore not true. This is sad, because it blinds us not only to the richness of human experience, but also to the possibility that science itself may function as a myth, in so far as we draw truths out of science that are beyond the so-called scientific facts themselves. Although in the last decade or so there has been a reaction against the poverty imposed on modern language, this reaction is as yet no more than a fringe affair; witness the utter incredulity recently expressed by a working class schoolchild when a highly educated friend of mine suggested to him there was often more truth in fairy stories than in the news.

It is therefore appropriate that the Bible should begin by sketching the paradoxical human condition and that, in doing so, it should use a story of the kind that modern anthropologists would call mythical. Contemporary theologians are rediscovering the insights to be found in the first few chapters of Genesis, and it is here that we will focus our discussion of the Judaic-Christian view of man and society. The reader should forget, hard though it may be for some, the tiresome wrangling of past generations over the relation of Genesis to the scientific theory of evolution. If we had to assess every human statement in terms of its conformity to the canons of modern science before it could be deemed of value, then there would be very little left worth saying. Certainly not much of modern science itself would remain!

No, whatever else the early chapters of Genesis are,

they are a prologue to the first five books of the Bible and also to the whole of the Bible itself[1]. They introduce the main characters for the whole drama of history as seen in the Jewish-Christian tradition. Among these actors are God, man and the natural world. Inevitably these appear in other religions and in other myths, so the aim of Genesis is to sketch briefly the particular kind of God, the particular nature of man and the particular place of nature that condition the biblical drama. Genesis is a serious attempt to state who man is, so that we may get on with understanding history – the history not only of Israel but of all mankind and of God's salvation. As with the introduction of the actors in a play, the object is not to prove scientifically what is stated. Rather it is to set the scene so that we may get on with the play; the critic bides his time till he has seen and, as far as he feels able, entered into the spirit of the rest of the play.

Even if the reader is not particularly interested in the history of ancient Israel and is sceptical about the Bible as revelation, the early chapters of Genesis still merit attention as a surprisingly enduring attempt by man to come to terms with the puzzle of himself. No other story of similar antiquity has been so influential on western culture, and even if one supposes this influence to have been detrimental or perverted one can hardly deny its importance. It will be argued here that this story not only starts off the history of ancient Israel, but also has some insights that prove remarkably helpful in orienting the study of modern society.

A Tale of Homelessness

At home in the world

The Genesis story starts in the first two chapters by placing mankind: the human person was created to have a place in relation to God, in relation to nature and in relation to other persons. In relation to God, we are made in his image. No one seems quite sure exactly what this means, but certainly the phrase asserts the nobility of mankind. We are not nothing, we have an importance that consists simply in our being; whatever we may or may not achieve, however other people treat us, we are still important and have worth in the eyes of God the ultimate giver of worth.

In relation to the natural world, the story first of all places us alongside nature in that we, like the rest of nature, are creatures; our physical existence and form is given and we are subject to the laws of nature. At the same time, though, man is portrayed as having dominion over the rest of nature, thus recognising and affirming our dual relation to nature, but putting it in a particularly positive light. Our dominion over nature is not such that we are responsible only to ourselves, a perilous view, for it allows us to decide for ourselves that economic gain is our primary goal, resulting in the wholesale exploitation of nature with the inevitable consequences. Nor are we responsible to nature itself as some modern ecologists would have it, for this begs the question of how we know what it is that nature would have of us and human history demonstrates the self-interested flexibility with which human beings have drawn moral lessons from nature. No, the Genesis story says that dominion over nature is granted by God, and therefore we are responsible to Him.

Thirdly, the story places one person in relation to another. It recognises the paradox that we identify ourselves both as individuals and as members of a species or community; we cannot define 'Man' as either singular or plural (emphases added):

> 'So God created man in his own image, in the image of God he created *him*; male and female he created *them*'[2]

This extraordinary sentence cuts through all the ideology, all the philosophy and all the wars that have been waged between those who believed in the individual and those who believed in the group and the nation. It recognises that the human person experiences individuality, yet is related to a group. It also cuts through the argument whether mankind is more truly typified by the male or the female:

> 'So God created *man* in his own image, in the image of God he created him; *male and female* he created them.'

The story of the creation of Eve recognises that a person is not fully human while alone, and becomes complete only in relationship with other persons. The individual is complete only within community.

There is one thread in the story which links the three topics of man's place in relation to God, to nature and to fellow humans, and this is that in each case having a place depends on God. Human nobility derives from our being in the image of God, not from any achievements of our own; keeping a place in relation to the natural world depends on a sense of responsibility to God rather than to nature or to ourselves. The next part of the story – the eating of the prohibited fruit of the tree of the knowledge of good and evil – declares that when man tries to exclude God then things go wrong in relationship both with other humans and with nature. When he rejected the command not to eat of this tree, the one prohibition in an otherwise totally rule-less world, Adam symbolised mankind's rejection of God as the creator and sustainer of all things, not least as the sustainer of man's home in the universe.

Eating the fruit of the tree symbolised man's attempt to 'go it alone', his determination to be autonomous and independent of God. Genesis goes on to tell how this had unanticipated consequences for mankind, and these are described in chapters 3 and 4 through the story of the fall of Adam and Eve and the story of Cain. Each of the consequences produced a new situation with which man had to come to terms[3].

Fugitives and wanderers

Firstly, both Adam and Cain in turn were made homeless. Adam and Eve were driven out of the garden of Eden, while their son Cain was made a fugitive and a wanderer for the murder of his brother Abel. Both Adam and Cain were no longer at home in the world. This Genesis image of human beings as wanderers on the face of the earth, and none too happy at that, corresponds to the homelessness theme in this book.

The story says that Cain dealt with his undesirable and unsettled state by building a city and starting a family. He coped with his rootlessness by putting down roots, and it is not too fanciful to suggest that here lies the human (as opposed to any divine) basis of the family and of the city. Man, intended to be free to respond to the goodness of God in creation, now finds himself building and propagating out of dire necessity. The world had collapsed all around Cain, and so he started the task of building up a new world of his own. Central to this task was controlling the social environment by starting a family, by having children whom he could mould and bring up to sustain what he had started. The city and the family represent the heart of human society and culture, and the essential similarity between building a city and starting a family is suggested by the fact that Cain called both the city and his son by the same name, Enoch. 'Enoch' means to dedicate, to inaugurate, to initiate, and so the city and the family are the first and key elements in Cain's project of starting up a society of his own, without God.

In this respect then, the Genesis story confirms the view of modern humanism that society is made by man for man. It also raises doubts about the completeness of the conventional 'Christian' view of the family as a divine institution. For Cain at any rate, it was nothing of the sort; rather it was a necessary way of confirming his home-made place in the universe, his chosen way of trying to mitigate the fugitive condition that resulted from cutting himself off from his Maker and Sustainer.

A second condition of human existence mentioned in the story of the Fall is death. Again, Adam and Eve's response is to try to mitigate the condition. Adam immediately calls his wife by the name Eve 'because she was the mother of all living', and thereby gave them both a stake in the future; even if they were to die, they could live on through their descendants. Likewise with Cain, his raising of a family and building of a city were ways of ensuring that something of him would extend beyond his personal death. It is significant that this profound story about the human condition does not neglect to mention man's mortality, and even more significant that the human response is portrayed as social. Social institutions (like the family) and human culture (embodied in the city) are ways in which we try to mitigate the conditions of homelessness and mortality; ways in which mankind tries to live with its fallen nobility.

A third result of the fall that the Genesis story presents is a breaking of the relationship of mankind to the natural world and the introduction of suffering. Adam is cursed with soil that will yield its fruit only if he toils and sweats for it. Perhaps Adam thought that once he was free of God's restriction then he would be free to exploit the earth, responsible to no-one but himself; but he found that once he set himself up as the autonomous master of nature, then nature ceased to co-operate. Similarly, Eve found that the natural function of childbirth was to become as sweaty and toilsome a business as Adam's labours in the fields.

The toilsome relationship with nature forces human beings to spend much of their time and ingenuity and much collaborative effort in feeding and clothing themselves. Emphasising the basic importance of the economics of need has been one of the major contributions of Marxism. Marx and Engels criticised the notion that history is totally shaped by ideas and by 'great men', and argued for a materialist conception of history:

> 'The first premise of all human existence, and, therefore, of all history (is) that men must be in a position to live in order to be able to 'make history'. Life involves before everything else eating and drinking, a habitation, clothing and many other things. The first historical act is thus the production of the means to satisfy these needs. . . . Therefore in any interpretation of history one has first of all to observe this fundamental fact in all its significance and all its implications and to accord it its due importance.'[4]

One does not need to be a thoroughgoing economic determinist to see that the need to subsist has widespread cultural as well as horticultural implications. For example, nomadic hunting tribes feed themselves in a way that demands co-operation among a small group of adult males and prevents the accumulation of much property. As a result, such societies tend to be relatively egalitarian (among the men at least). Also marriage is arranged so that the woman leaves her kinship group and joins the man's in order not to break up the closely-knit group of male hunters. Thus economics profoundly influences social structure.

Another important detail in the Genesis story is that conflict between one human being and another is associated with the production of food: Cain was jealous of his brother's offering to God. Not only is producing the material means of life an act of religious significance, but it is also a toilsome affair so that if food is in short supply conflict will result. Much time has to be invested in food production, and it is not surprising that Cain felt bitter when after all his sweat and toil in the fields his harvest was not deemed acceptable.

Genesis shows that human culture has become the means by which mankind solves the problems of the fall – homelessness, mortality, suffering and a disrupted relation to nature.

Sin and Social Order

The Genesis story suggests how the sociological picture of society portrayed in this book may be placed within a much broader drama. Genesis implies that human culture, intended by God as a means by which mankind can participate in the continuous act of creation, has become instead a response to problems inherent in the fallen nobility of man. Mankind, breaking away from God, finds itself alone in the universe, homeless and naked. Adam and Eve are described as covering up their nakedness with fig leaves and trying to hide from God, but Cain's building a city and raising a family represent a more comprehensive (and crucially a sociological rather than a physiological) cover-up job. The city and family provided both a set of meanings and a project that protected Cain from the nothingness outside of God. Cain (like Adam and Eve) had plunged himself into chaos, for he had wrecked the order provided by God; the terror of chaos is something human beings do their utmost to protect themselves from. This was the significance of family and city for Cain: they protected him from the terror and the chaos outside God. In fact, the whole human drama can be understood in these terms; intended by God as a free response to the challenge to relate to nature and to each other, culture has become a means of protecting mankind from God. Its panorama of meaning and activity covers up our nakedness. This is why there is a tension throughout the Bible between God and human society; from the prophets through Jesus and on to the Book of Revelation we find a running critique of human institutions as human creations set up in place of God[5].

Theologically, this book has explored the implications for social order of the traditional doctrine of sin. It has interpreted social order in terms of man the sinner trying to carve out a new place for himself now that he has rejected his creator. It has hinted that God may sometimes intend to disturb the 'idols' and the 'home' that constitute the social order.

This linking of social order with sin, and disruption with God, may surprise or even disturb some Christian readers. Western Christians commonly assume the association to be the other way around – that social order is from God and conflict of the devil. Social order is seen as part of God's common grace; family, work and the state are often believed to be ordained and sustained by God, while industrial strikes, political rebellion and other forms of conflict are assumed to be the result of sin (ch.10).

Christians who believe in a neat 'order is of God, conflict of the devil' formulation would do well to ponder that in countries where Christians are not so materially and politically benefited by the social order as in the west this neat distinction is implausible. Thus black Christians in South Africa, Baptists in the USSR, and German members of the Confessing Church during the Second

World War, took it for granted that the social order is not wholly from God.

Throughout the Bible, God is portrayed as confusing the social order rather than bolstering it up. Thus in the story of the building of the Tower of Babel[6] in which the tower is a symbol of man's pride and attempted independence of God, God's response is to scatter and confuse the builders. Similarly in the New Testament, the Magnificat asserts that God 'has scattered the proud in the imagination of their hearts'. Several Old Testament prophets interpreted the defeat of the Israelite nation at the hands of outside invaders as the action of a jealous God scattering those who had set themselves up over against him. The theme running through all this is that man is an essentially proud being who creates order by putting himself at the centre and glorifying himself through national and civic pride, while God periodically intervenes to shatter this.

In this view, the roots of social order lie in the rebellious religious nature of man; this contrasts not only with the view of many Christians who believe that social order is necessarily of God, but also with contemporary humanism which denies the religious nature of social life. This is not to suggest that chaos is in itself a good thing, but that chaos can be a divine means to a new and better order.

The sociological significance of the fall

Christian theology sees the human drama as a fourfold process of Creation, Fall, Redemption and Christ's coming again. 1) God's creation is wholly good and offers mankind a life of freedom and security. 2) Mankind forfeits this through wanting to be independent of God, and so society as we know it is the product of fallen human activity within the limits set up in creation. 3) Christ offers redemption through his death and resurrection. 4) There is a coming age which will totally embody the kingdom of God. For the purpose of understanding society as it is now, i.e. for the purpose of a descriptive sociology, the relevant theological doctrines are those of Creation and Fall. Why then has this book focused on the significance for sociology of the Fall to the neglect of Creation? There are several reasons.

Firstly, sociology has become imbued with an optimism that comports badly with its humanism. Modern sociology is correctly humanistic in that it sees society as an essentially human construction[7], but in general it fails to see the way in which human society is the vehicle for Man's rebellion against his Maker. Indeed, this notion is specifically rejected in one popular book on the sociology of the family (published in the early 1960s) which criticises the legacy of St. Augustine for whom 'all human institutions were essentially sinful, and redeemed only by the grace of God'[8]. Yet this is a curious criticism to come in a book whose back cover asserts that 'history is largely a long tale of poverty, drudgery, desertion, and vagrancy'. If this is what history teaches sociology, how can the sociologist believe that modern society has miraculously transcended the hitherto universal human lot?

The answer has much to do with the circumstances that gave rise to the expansion of modern sociology in the 1960s. In the decade or two following the destruction of World War II when industrial societies literally had to build a new world, mankind came to believe (perhaps given the enormity of the task, *had* to believe) that it was basically good and had within itself the power, as never before, to shape its own future. Affluence, technology and democracy had at last given mankind the tools for autonomy. Sociology shared in this optimism; governments enthusiastically funded sociological research while students flocked to study the subject that would provide man with control over his own destiny.

But as noted in ch. 6, this myth of progress was undermined among the middle classes and especially among students and intellectuals from the mid 1960s onwards as technological society proved incapable of ushering in the promised utopia. Sociology in the 1970s reflected this general undermining of optimism and began to grope for a new style and a new framework[9]; its humanism remained, but its optimism wore pretty thin. In this situation, sociology is in need of a philosophy that rejects the myth of progress but that still retains as central the tenet that society is a *human* enterprise. This means that the theological doctrine of the Fall is of great relevance to modern sociology.

Secondly, this book has focused on the Fall rather than on Creation because this is what Christians as well as sociologists need to be made aware of. Those many Christians who have become social activists tend to look to the doctrines of creation and the kingdom to provide their social activism with a biblical rationale. They believe society to be part of God's creation and therefore a fit setting for Christian discipleship (compare the discussion of the Protestant ethic in ch. 2), or that political change is the means by which the Kingdom of God will come on earth. There is much truth in the first and perhaps a little in the second of these assertions, and they are undoubtedly effective as *motivations* for political commitment and social action. But by themselves they are very far from a theology of society for they ignore at least half of the Christian message. In particular, they ignore the necessity that in order to understand society as it is (as opposed to its nature in God's mind before time began or as it may be at the end of time) there must be some appreciation of mankind as fallen. The result is that Christians' comprehension of society is often grotesquely naive and appallingly utopian. There is more than a trace here of Christians absorbing wholesale from the surrounding culture the optimistic myth of progress.

The third reason why a theology of society today is most in need of the doctrine of the Fall is that the more traditionally minded Christians who still believe that man is fallen tend to hold this belief in a very individualistic way. They speak as if sin resided solely within the individual and individual salvation were the only message and concern of the gospel. They will not be dissuaded from this misunderstanding by a theology of society that does not give full recognition to the fall.

It is in this context, where sociologists and Christians alike fail to recognise the importance of either society or human fallenness (or both), that this book deliberately lacks balance and focuses on society as a response to the problems of fallen humanity. It has talked of the family, work and so on as idols, because this is what both sociologists and Christians most need to understand: sociologists need to know that these social institutions and movements are inherently religious, while both they and Christians need to know that social institutions (whatever else they may be) are also manifestations of human fallenness.

It should be clear, however, that this interpretation does not exhaust the significance of family, work, etc. In the Judaic-Christian view, the whole of human culture is intended by God to be entered into and opened up freely, but this freedom has been replaced by human *dependence* on social institutions which are deemed to be the source of life and meaning. Since the social has become sacred, the individual is dependent not on his Creator but on the creation, with all the potential for exploitation and conflict that has been alluded to in ch. 10. The Christian gospel opens up the possibility of freedom, provided that we stop looking for the ultimate within society, within the individual self or within nature. This Christian truth corresponds to a well-known sociological insight. It is what Max Weber describes as Judaism's and Christianity's tendency to 'disenchant' the world; they banish the sacred from society, from nature and from politics, and it is precisely because of this banishment that they enable human beings to become social beings and explore the world in freedom[10].

Idolatry

So we return to the theme of idolatry. The Judaic-Christian tradition does not object to nature, society, technology or human-ness per se (although the recurrent heresy of gnosticism does just this), but to their elevation to the sacred. The crucial distinction according to this tradition is not the difference between the religious and the irreligious (a distinction which much concerns contemporary sociologists of religion who want to carve out a definable area of study), for in the biblical view all of life is religious and to be a human being inevitably means to be a worshipping being. The crucial distinction is whether worship is directed to the true God or to some false god

– truly directed or idolatrously directed. No distinction is made between false gods that claim supernatural powers and those that are immanent within the world (thus in the biblical view the supernatural-natural distinction is of little importance for the understanding of religion). Anything (purportedly human or superhuman) that competes for man's adoration is an idol and religiously directed away from God; all such competitors are really only human fabrications, upon which people of insight from the prophets of old to Karl Marx have poured scorn.

Hence the implicitly critical tone in this book's analysis of the sacred in modern (or indeed of any) society. Sociologically speaking, the sacred today is a fact; theologically speaking, it is to be deplored.

Images of Man

The theme of mankind in self-imposed exile, alone in the universe and autonomous of God, has pervaded not only this book but also Christianity itself and its cultural heir, western civilisation. But the image of Man associated with homelessness can vary. There are three images which find an echo in this book – the stoic, the defiant and the pathetic – and the echo gets stronger as we move through the three. Let us look at each.

Stoicism

This is the classic stance of the agnostic or atheist humanist. Man is alone in the universe facing absurdity; there is no meaning 'out there' to be discovered or revealed, and mankind has no option but to create its own meaning. Morality is concerned with whether this is faced with stoicism and equanimity or with alienation and a whimper[11]. Given the futility of fallen existence, one cannot but have a certain respect for the lengths to which human beings have gone to construct a social world of their own in the face of absurdity.

Defiance

Past generations have seen a very different image looming large in the church. This image agrees that human beings want nothing to do with God, but goes on to portray this as an act of defiance. Man is not just on his own but also a sinner defiantly waving his fist at God and shouting 'I can do without you.' The church's response to this image has often been to proclaim judgment and retribution on Man the Wilful Sinner.

This book has modified this image by presenting the canopy that human beings erect to keep God out as primarily *social*. It is society that provides the umbrella of meanings which renders fallen existence tolerable. If judgment is part of the message of Christianity, it is to be directed at human culture as much as at the human individual. Thus a Judaic-Christian approach to sociology leads on to cultural criticsm, as we have already seen in discussing the theme of idolatry. To describe the sacred in society as 'idolatrous' implies criticism and judgement.

But the Christian tradition includes another theme related to this one of defiance, for God is portrayed not only as the distant God thundering against human iniquity, but also as the God who himself took on human flesh. The theme of Man's defiance is superseded by that of God's acceptance of Man.

Nowhere are the sociological implications of this better drawn than in the biblical treatment of the city[12]. From Cain onwards, the city is portrayed as a shield built by man against the terror and chaos of life without God. It has Man as its focal point, and the glorification of Man as its aim. The story of the building of the Tower of Babel depicts human beings building a city in order 'to make a name for themselves', to glorify themselves and declare their power. It will be a home of their very own. But although the city represents mankind's rejection of God, this theme is gradually superseded in the Bible by another theme that God, far from rejecting the human city, has actually adopted it. God has chosen man's choice. This is shown in God's adoption of the city of Jerusalem as the location for the Temple, the holy place that symbolised his presence. The city, the very place from which man wanted to exclude God, has been re-entered by him. Man finds he cannot escape God in the city after all, and is confronted once again with the frailty of his condition and with his status as a homeless wanderer looking for somewhere to hide from the face of God.

The special role of Jerusalem became redundant once God declared his presence on earth in Jesus Christ. Once again the city could not stand the presence of God, and the crucifixion represents the supreme attempt of the city to rid itself of the presence of God. Jesus was prepared to accomplish his salvation in the city, but the city would have none of it and crucified him outside the city walls. Although the city has rejected God, he has not rejected the city. God's refusal to do this is seen in the Book of Revelation in which heaven is depicted as a city, albeit a somewhat verdant and pastoral city. It is this constant biblical theme of God's willingness to declare his presence in the city, to meet us at the very point of our rejection of him, that provides hope in the possibility of the renewal of the city, hope that it is worth working for and loving. And what goes for the city, goes also for the whole of human culture. But like the city, it may crucify us in the process.

Pathos

A third image associated with the theme of homelessness represents human beings huddled together for security to protect themselves from the absurdity of fallen existence. The image is not of the *individual* cuddled up with his fantasies, but of the social huddle that keeps these fantasies plausible.

The image here is one of pathos. The criminologist David Matza[13] has argued that the notion of pathology (the belief that the criminal has done something wrong), although possibly useful for other purposes, does not help us understand the meaning the criminal gives his actions. An appreciation of the pathos in his existence, by contrast, is essential if we are to comprehend it properly. This book has extended this notion from criminology to sociology to suggest that an appreciation of its pathetic elements is essential if the human condition is to be properly understood. Traditional Christian theology has emphasised human pathology, which points to the judgement of God; this book, though, has advocated an appreciation of human pathos, which points to the plight of man.

The aim of this book, then, is to portray the human condition as manifested in society, and to foster a response that is neither that of stoicism nor that of anger and condemnation. Instead, as one looks at the existence endured by human beings alienated from God and at the proliferation of sacred objects to which we have enslaved ourselves, the appropriate response can only be pity. It is this pathos of the human condition that I have tried to express and explain.

This may be viewed askance by sociologists who see their task as the dispassionate, objective and scientific analysis of society. But science is not totally lacking in passion, values and commitments; indeed it ultimately rests on such things[14]. It is therefore reasonable to explore what modern sociology could look like when combined with the radical monotheism of Christianity, which is what this book has attempted. The resulting analysis of society is neither superficial nor merely subjective and personal. Rather, it draws on two publicly available languages of historic and contemporary importance for modern society – Christianity and sociology – neither of which can be reasonably ignored in the search for an understanding of the perplexing world we live in.

Notes

CHAPTER ONE (pages 9–24)

1. For a discussion of the various ways in which sociologists have defined secularisation, see L. SHINER, 'The Meanings of Secularisation', *International Yearbook for the Sociology of Religion*, Vol. 3, 1967.
2. David MARTIN, *A General Theory of Secularization*, Oxford: Blackwell (1978); Peter BERGER, *The Social Reality of Religion*, London: Faber (1969).
3. See, in Britain, the work of Bryan WILSON, e.g. *Contemporary Transformations of Religion*, Oxford University Press (1976).
4. There are a few exceptions. David Martin challenged the usefulness of the concept in 'Towards Eliminating the Concept of Secularisation' in J. GOULD (ed), *Penguin Survey of the Social Sciences*, Harmondsworth: Penguin (1965), but then proceeded to write *A General Theory of Secularization* (op. cit.)! Peter GLASNER, *The Sociology of Secularisation: a critique of a concept*, London: Routledge (1977) argues that the notion is ideological rather than scientific.
5. P. BERGER, *The Social Reality of Religion*, op. cit.
6. Bryan WILSON, *Religion in Secular Society*, London: Watts (1966), p. xiv.
7. See for example, Peter BERGER, *A Rumour of Angels*, Harmondsworth: Pelican (1971), ch. 1.
8. No claims are made that this definition of the sacred is universal or applicable to non-western societies. For this, see the several works on the sacred by anthropologists, e.g. Emile DURKHEIM, *The Elementary Forms of the Religious Life*, London: Allen and Unwin (1976), pp. 36–42 and his many critics; Michael BANTON (ed), *Anthropological Approaches to the Study of Religion*, London: Tavistock (1966); Mary DOUGLAS, *Purity and Danger*, Harmondsworth: Penguin (1970); and the work of French structuralists such as Lèvi-Strauss. These studies stress the relation between the sacred and the profane which is underplayed in this book.

9. Paul TILLICH has drawn attention to this aspect of the sacred.
10. Roland ROBERTSON, *The Sociological Interpretation of Religion*, Oxford: Blackwell (1970) criticises the idea that religion involves ultimate commitment as itself religious and not scientifically neutral. This begs the question of the possibility of a neutral social science. See also Melford E. SPIRO, 'Religion: problems of definition and explanation', pp. 85–126 in M. BANTON, op. cit. who notes usefully that ultimate commitments in traditional tribal religions may be oriented to this world (health, wealth, etc.) rather than to supernatural beings which are perceived simply as instrumental to these worldly ends.
11. See e.g. P. BERGER, *The Social Reality of Religion*, op. cit., and Clifford GEERTZ, 'Religion as a Cultural System', pp. 1–46 in M. BANTON, op. cit.
12. See Max WEBER, *The Sociology of Religion*, New York: Beacon Press (1964).
13. The classic statement is by DURKHEIM in *The Elementary Forms of the Religious Life*, op. cit.
14. E. SHORTER, *The Making of the Modern Family*, London: Fontana (1977).
15. E. DURKHEIM, *Elementary Forms*, op. cit. For a good discussion of the relation between Durkheim's and Marx's views on religion, see R. ROBERTSON, op. cit., pp. 19–21. Also on society as religion, T. LUCKMANN, *The Invisible Religion*, New York: MacMillan (1967).
16. Erich FROMM, 'Karl Marx's Theory of Alienation', pp. 188–196 in D. H. WRONG & H. L. GRACEY (eds), *Readings in Introductory Sociology*, New York: MacMillan (1972).
17. Herbert MARCUSE, *One Dimensional Man*, London: Routledge (1964). See also ch. 10.
18. W. KOLB, 'Images of Man and the Sociology of Religion', *Journal for the Scientific Study of Religion*, 1(1), Oct. 1961, p. 14.
19. This is the American title of *The Social Reality of Religion*, op. cit. See also, LUCKMANN, op. cit., and P. BERGER & Thomas LUCKMANN, *The Social Construction of Reality*, London: Allen Lane (1967).
20. Contrary to popular misunderstanding, Weber emphasised both sides of this coin. See e.g. his *General Economic History*, New York: Collier Books (1961), pp. 258–270, as well as the better known *The Protestant Ethic and the Spirit of Capitalism*, London: Unwin (1930).
21. E. DURKHEIM, *The Division of Labour in Society*, New York: Free Press (1964); *Suicide*, New York: Free Press (1952).
22. See the work of structuralist anthropologists, e.g. Lèvi-Srauss.

23. Geoffrey GORER, *Death, Grief and Mourning in Contemporary Britain*, London: Cresset Press (1965).
24. Philippe ARIES, *Western Attitudes Toward Death: from the Middle Ages to the Present*, Baltimore: John Hopkins Univ. Press (1974).

CHAPTER TWO (pages 25–46)

1. M. WEBER, *The Protestant Ethic*, op. cit.
2. E. P. THOMPSON, *The Making of the English Working Class*, Harmondsworth: Penguin (1968).
3. P. BERGER, 'Some General Observations on the Problem of Work', in *The Human Shape of Work*, New York: MacMillan (1964).
4. F. MUSGROVE, *Ecstasy and Holiness – counter culture and the open society*, London: Methuen (1974), pp. 178–9.
5. D. RIESMAN, *The Lonely Crowd*, New York: Yale Univ. Press (1961), pp. 280–3.
6. V. FRANKL, *The Doctor and the Soul*, New York: Knopf (1961), pp. 111–2. Christians who continue their weekday tempo into a Sunday which they fill with all kinds of church meetings and activities would do well to question any lack of sympathy for non-church-going friends who find Sunday such a bore. Many Christians may be so busy on Sunday, not so much in the service of their Lord, but because they too cannot face letting up for a moment and find church activities a convenient way out.
7. See Bill JORDAN, *Freedom and the Welfare State*, London: Routledge (1976), ch. 14; and Haddon WILLMER, *Towards a Theology of Politics*, Nottingham: Shaftesbury Project (1976).
8. W. A. JOHNSON, 'The Guaranteed Income as an Environmental Measure', ch. 8 in H. E. DALY (ed), *Toward a Steady-State Economy*, San Francisco: W. H. Freeman (1973), p. 184.
9. Advert in *Radio Times*, 14th April 1978.
10. Mary DOUGLAS, 'Why Do People Want Goods?', *The Listener*, 8th Sept. 1977, pp. 292–3.
11. JORDAN, op. cit., ch. 13.

CHAPTER THREE (pages 47–66)

1. This suggests why individualistic Christians are rather more common than socially involved ones, for they are simply following the fashion and adopting the easiest way of coping with an alienating society by retreating into a private and personal world.
2. P. BERGER & H. KELLNER, 'Marriage and the Construction of Reality', *Diogenes*, 46 (1964), pp. 1–25.

3. P. ARIES, *Western Attitudes Toward Death*, op. cit., p. 92.
4. P. ARIES, *Centuries of Childhood*, London: Cape (1962), p. 9.
5. E. SHORTER, op. cit., p. 16.
6. However, these church ceremonies do offer the clergy opportunities to meet unchurched parishioners.
7. Juan Luis SEGUNDO, *Our Idea of God*, Vol 3 of *A Theology for Artisans of a New Humanity*, Maryknoll, New York: Orbis Books (1974), pp. 67–8.
8. Lewis MUMFORD, *The City in History*, London: Secker & Warburg (1961), p. 383.
9. David CLINES, 'Social Responsibility in the Old Testament', *Interchange*, 20 (1976), pp. 195–6.
10. R. FOX, *Kinship and Marriage*, Harmondsworth: Penguin (1967).
11. SHORTER, op. cit., p. 17.

CHAPTER FOUR (pages 67–84)

1. DOUGLAS, 'Why Do People Want Goods?', op. cit.
2. J. REX & R. MOORE, *Race, Community and Conflict*, Oxford Univ. Press (1969).
3. S. COHEN AND L. TAYLOR, *Escape Attempts: the theory and practice of resistance to everyday life*, London: Allen Lane (1976).
4. I am exploring images of the countryside, especially of wild and natural countryside, in a forthcoming book.

CHAPTER FIVE (pages 85–102)

1. J. ELLUL, *Propaganda*, New York: Vintage (1973), ch. 3.
2. Emil BRUNNER, *Love and Marriage* (selections from *The Divine Imperative*), London: Fontana (1970), p. 128.
3. ELLUL, *Propaganda*, op. cit., p. 92.
4. E. GOFFMAN, *Asylums*, Harmondsworth: Penguin (1968) is a classic account of how in a welfare state people protect their individuality by developing an underworld of their own.
5. Jacob BURCKHARDT, *The Civilisation of the Renaissance in Italy*, New York: Mentor (1960), pp. 128–134.
6. See the work of the so-called labelling theorists, e.g. H. BECKER, *Outsiders*, New York: Free Press (1963).
7. See, for example, the popular books of R. D. Laing.
8. See BURCKHARDT, op. cit., & ARIES, *Western Attitudes Towards Death*, op. cit.
9. BRUNNER, op. cit., pp. 124–5.

CHAPTER SIX (pages 103–119)

1. J. ELLUL, *The New Demons*, Oxford: Mowbrays (1976), ch. 4.
2. See the forthcoming book referred to in note 4, ch. 4.
3. THE ECOLOGIST, *A Blueprint for Survival*, Harmondsworth: Penguin (1972), p. 19.
4. M. BOOKCHIN, 'Ecology and Revolutionary Thought', in R. CLARKE (ed), *Notes for the Future*, London: Thames & Hudson (1975).
5. K. BOULDING, 'The Economics of the Coming Spaceship Earth', in H. JARRETT (ed), *Environmental Quality in a Growing Economy*, Baltimore: Johns Hopkins Univ. Press (1966)
6. R. NEUHAUS, *In Defense of People – ecology and the seduction of radicalism*, New York: Macmillan (1970) provides a stimulating critique of modern ecological ideas from a broadly biblical position.
7. D. MEADOWS et al, *The Limits to Growth*, London: Earth Island (1972).
8. R. HOOYKAAS, *Religion and the Rise of Modern Science*, Edinburgh: Scottish Academic Press (1972), and R. K. MERTON, 'Puritanism, pietism and science', in *Social Theory and Social Structure*, New York: Free Press (1964).
9. The classic statement of this view is L. WHITE Jr., 'The Historical Roots of Our Ecologic Crisis', *Science*, March 1967.
10. A. HUXLEY, 'The Politics of Population', *The Center Magazine* (Santa Barbara, California) March 1969.
11. T. DALE & V. CARTER, *Topsoil and Civilsation*, Univ. of Oklahoma Press (1974).
12. D. OWEN, *What is Ecology?*, London: Oxford University Press (1974), pp. v-vi.
13. M. ALLABY, *Inventing the Future*, London: Hodder (1976), p. 71.
14. L. WHITE Jr., 'Continuing the Conversation', in I. G. BARBOUR (ed), *Western Man and Environmental Ethics*, Mass: Addison-Wesley (1973).
15. P. FLEISCHMAN, 'Conservation, the Biological Fallacy', *Landscape*, 18 (1969), pp. 23–7.
16. E. WATT, *Principles of Environmental Science*, New York: McGraw Hill (1973).

CHAPTER SEVEN (pages 120–137)

1. H. HONOUR, *The New Golden Land: European images of America from the discoveries to the present time*, New York: Pantheon (1975).
2. ELLUL, *Propaganda*, op. cit., p. 155.
3. Reported in *The Guardian*, 31st Jan. 1978, p. 22.

4. ELLUL, *Propaganda*, op. cit., p. 160.
5. M. MULLER, *Aboriginal Issues: More Facts and Figures*, Geneva: World Council of Churches, Program to Combat Racism (1971).
6. F. ENGEL, *Turning Land Into Hope: towards a new Aboriginal policy for Australia*, Sydney: Australian Council of Churches (1969), p. 12.
7. A. KUYPER, *Lectures on Calvinism*, Grand Rapids: Associated Publishers (no date).
8. SEGUNDO, op. cit., p. 65. See Genesis ch. 11, and The Acts of the Apostles, ch. 2.

CHAPTER EIGHT (pages 138–151)

1. This chapter is a modified form of 'Violence and Unreason', *Third Way*, 8th Sept. 1977.
2. Stuart HALL, 'A World At One With Itself', *New Society*, 18th June 1970, pp. 1056–8.
3. GLASGOW MEDIA GROUP, *Bad News*, London: Routledge (1976).
4. See Tony WALTER, 'Emotional Disturbance: what does it mean?', *Social Work Today*, 8 (29), 26th April 1977, pp. 8–10.
5. J. ELLUL, *Violence*, New York: Seabury Press (1969).
6. See e.g. R. D. LAING, *The Divided Self*, London: Tavistock (1960).
7. ELLUL, *Violence*, op. cit.
8. John V. TAYLOR, 'A Church Reshaped', *Christian*, 3 (2), 1975–6, p. 109.

CHAPTER NINE (pages 152–169)

1. P. BERGER & R. NEUHAUS, *Against the World for the World*, New York: Seabury (1976).
2. DURKHEIM, *Elementary Forms*, op. cit.
3. CLINES, op. cit.
4. Michel QUOIST, *Prayers of Life*, Dublin: Gill (1966).
5. Matthew 19:23; 8:19–22; 10:35–39; 5:10–11; 1 Corinthians 1:18–25.
6. Quoted in H. R. NIEBUHR, *The Social Sources of Denominationalism*, New York: Meridian (1957).
7. NIEBUHR, op. cit., p. 9.
8. F. SCHAEFFER, *The Mark of the Christian*, Leicester: Inter-Varsity Press (1971), pp. 13–14.
9. For an elaboration of this view of war, see ELLUL, *Violence*, op. cit.
10. A. J. AYER, *Language, Truth and Logic*, London: Gollancz (1936).
11. For a fuller critique of Cox along these lines, see ELLUL,

New Demons, op. cit.

12. D. MOBERG, *The Great Reversal – evangelism versus social concern*, London: Scripture Union (1973).
13. E.g. James Callaghan in *The Daily Telegraph*, 23rd May 1978.

CHAPTER TEN (pages 170–184)

1. See the critique of liberation theology and social action in ch. 9. Also, Edward NORMAN, *Christianity and the World Order*, Oxford University Press, 1979.
2. MARCUSE, op. cit.
3. For an analysis of the operation of social work, see J. A. WALTER, *Sent Away: a study of young offenders in care*, Farnborough: Saxon House (1978).
4. Quoted in V. ELLER, *The Simple Life: the Christian view of possessions*, London: Hodder (1974), p. 81.

CHAPTER ELEVEN (pages 185–201)

1. G. VON RAD, *Genesis*, London: SCM (1972).
2. Genesis 1.27.
3. This section is greatly indebted to J. ELLUL, *The Meaning of the City*, Grand Rapids: Eerdmans (1970), especially ch. 1.
4. K. MARX & F. ENGELS, *The German Ideology*, London: Lawrence & Wishart (1965).
5. See also St. Paul's critique of 'the flesh' and 'the world' in which mankind seeks life in the creation rather than in the Creator, and hence misses life. R. BULTMANN, *Theology of the New Testament*, London: SCM (1952), pp. 232–246.
6. Genesis ch. 11.
7. For a good introductory statement see P. BERGER, *Invitation to Sociology: a humanistic perspective*, Harmondsworth: Penguin (1966).
8. R. FLETCHER, *The Family and Marriage in Modern Britain*, Harmondsworth: Penguin (1966).
9. For a good overview of the groupings of the late 1960s, see A. GOULDNER, *The Coming Crisis in Western Sociology*, New York: Basic Books (1970), and R. FRIEDRICHS, *A Sociology of Sociology*, New York: Free Press (1970).
10. This is strongly stated in Harvey COX'S otherwise highly problematic *The Secular City*, Harmondsworth: Penguin (1968). ELLUL, *The New Demons*, op. cit. correctly points to the historical fact that every major attempt at desacralisation (Christianity, the Reformation, Science) led in time to the setting up of new sacreds, which is what our analysis leads us to expect.
11. For an example of stoicism by two sociologists, see COHEN

& TAYLOR, op. cit.

12. See ELLUL, *The Meaning of the City*, op. cit.
13. David MATZA, *Becoming Deviant*, Englewood Cliffs: Prentice Hall (1970).
14. For classic statements of this view of science as committed, see Thomas KUHN, *The Structure of Scientific Revolutions*, University of Chicago Press (1962), and Michael POLANYI, *Personal Knowledge*, London: Routledge (1958).

Further Reading

References to books and articles on the various aspects of society discussed in chapters 2–10 are given in the notes. The following few works by Berger and Ellul may be of interest to anyone wanting to delve deeper into the overall framework outlined in chapters 1 and 11. They are listed by order of appearance in the text.

ELLUL, *The New Demons*, Mowbrays (1976)
A critique of the notion of secularisation, arguing that myths, symbols and the sacred are as alive as ever. Analyses the sacreds of technique, sex, the nation-state and revolution, and the myths of history and science.

BERGER, *Invitation to Sociology*, Penguin (1966)
Popular and lucid introduction to the sociological view of society as a human construction.

BERGER & LUCKMANN, *The Social Construction of Reality*, Allen Lane (1967)
Theoretical treatise, worth exploring if you already have some prior acquaintance with sociology or philosophy.

BERGER & KELLNER, 'Marriage and the Construction of Reality', *Diogenes*, 46 (1964), pp. 1–25. (Reprinted in various readers.)
Application of the social construction of reality thesis to the family, which is seen as an arena in which partners construct their private world.

ELLUL, *The Meaning of the City*, Eerdmans (1970)
Analysis of the biblical treatment of the city, which forms the basis for a Christian cultural criticism.

INDEX OF NAMES AND SUBJECTS

Authors' and people's names are in italics.
After references to items in the Notes section, the relevant pages in the text are shown in brackets.